Chariots of Gods or Demons?

The Incredible Truth

About

UFOs and Extraterrestrials

BY

JAMES EDWARD GILMER

STATION LIBRARY
BLDG 298 E ST
PSC BOX 8009
CHERRY POINT NC 28533

© 2002 by James Edward Gilmer. All rights reserved.

No part of this book may be reproduced, stored in a retrieval system, or transmitted by any means, electronic, mechanical, photocopying, recording, or otherwise, without written permission from the author.

ISBN: 0-7596-9356-0 (ebook)
ISBN: 0-7596-9357-9 (softcover)
ISBN: 0-7596-9358-7 (hardcover)

This book is printed on acid free paper.

1stBooks – rev. 4/10/02

Table of Contents

Chapter I: The Starting Point 1
What Are UFOs? 1
   My UFO Encounter 2
The Questions 3

Chapter 2: About UFO Sightings 7
Real or Hoax? 7
   An Impeccable Witness: New Hampshire, 1971 7
   A Prominent Witness: Georgia, 1969 7
   A Trusted Witness: Sweden, 1957 8
Close Encounters 9
Close Encounters of the Third Kind 10
   The Wave of 1973 10
   Valensole, France, 1965 12
   The "Socorro Affair", 1964 13
   The Wilcox Sighting, New York, 1964 14
Do UFOs Often Leave Solid Evidence of Their Presence? 15
   More Ground Depressions – Tennessee, 1973 15
   More Ground Depressions: Transylvania Alps, Romania, 1972 ... 16
   Steam and Perforated Ice in Bodies of Water– Cape Cod, 1971 .. 16
   Electrical Disturbances – Brazil, Illinois, 1957 17
   Other Power Station Outages – Brazil, 1959; New York, 1966 ... 17
Are UFOs Seen Mostly in America? 19
Are UFO Sightings Strictly a Modern Phenomenon? 19

Chapter 3: Why Have Aliens Been Visiting Us? 21
Patterns 21
  Geographic Areas 21
  Power Stations and Man-Made Aircraft 22
   Space Shuttle Columbia, Cape Canaveral 1996 22
  Places of Conflicts and Threats 22
   Afghanistan and Pakistan, Fall, 2001; August, 2000 23
   Ashland, Maine, 1999 23
   Operation Desert Fox, December 1998 24
   Nellis Air Force Base, Nevada, May 1997 24
   Ecuadorian Military Base, June 1996 25
   Israeli Flap of 1996 26
   The Belgian Flap of 1989-90 27

Fort Benning, Georgia, 1977 28
Iran, 1976 28
Fort Ritchie, Maryland, 1976 29
Cannon Air Force Base, New Mexico, 1976 29
Falconbridge Air Force Station, Ontario, Canada, 1975 30
Loring Air Force Base, Maine, 1975 30
Vandenburg Air Force Base, California, 1974 31
Mansfield, Ohio, 1973 32
Vietnam, 1968 32
Ellsworth Air Force Base, South Dakota, 1966 33
Edwards Air Force Base, California, 1965 34
Exeter, New Hampshire, 1965 34
Waltham, Massachusetts, 1964 36
Osan Air Force Base, Korea, 1961 36
Lakenheath, England, 1956 36
Fort Meade, Maryland, 1953-54 37
The UFO Mission: Observation, Intervention and Guardianship 38
Close Encounters of The Fourth Kind: Abductions 39
   Barney and Betty Hill, 1961 39
   England, 1980 43
   Argentina, 1975 44
   Parker and Hickson, 1973 45
   Alien Seduction? Brazil, 1957 45

Chapter 4: The Modern-Day Reappearance of UFOs 47
World War II Sightings 47
   Foo Fighters 48
   Gut Alt Gossen, Germany, 1944 49
Post-War UFO Activity 50
   Ghost Rockets, 1946-48 50
The Definitive Wave of the Modern Era: 1947-52 51
   The Roswell Crash, New Mexico, July, 1947 52
   The Mantell Case, Kentucky, 1948 56
   Southeast Asia, 1948 58
   New Mexico, 1948-50 58
   Oak Ridge, Tennessee, 1950 59
   An Astronaut's Sightings, Europe, 1951 59
   The Lubbock Lights, Texas, 1951 60
   The Wave of 1952 61
      The 1952 Flap Over Washington, D.C. 62
      NATO Exercises, English Channel, 1952 63

Chapter 5: Pre-Modern And Ancient Sightings 65
   The UFO Wave of 1896-97 66
   Turkey, 1885 67
   Northwest Africa, 1870 67
   London, 1742 67
   Nuremberg, 1561; Basel, 1566 68
   Japan, 1235 A.D. 68
   Gempeii War, Japan, 1180 69
   Jerusalem, 11th Century 69
   France, 8th-10th Centuries 69
   Charlemagne, 810 A.D. 70
   England, 776 A.D. 70
   Roman Empire, 1st-3rd Centuries B.C. 70
   Alexander the Great, 336 B.C.-323 B.C. 71
   Pharaoh Thutmose III, Egypt, 1469 B.C. 71
   Biblical UFO Sightings? 74
   Did Ezekiel See a UFO? 74
   Other UFO Sightings in the Bible? 80
   Would UFOs Contradict the Bible? 87

Chapter 6: Where Do UFOs Go? 89
Interdimensional Travel? 89
Black Holes, White Holes and Wormholes? 89
Closer to Home 90
   Which Planets and Moons? 91
     The Jovian Planets 91
     Jovian Moons 92
     The Terrestrial Planets 92
   The Habitable Zone 94
   The Enigmatic Moon 94
     The Moon's Origin 94
     A Watery Moon? 95
     A Hollow Moon? 96
   Artificial Structures on the Moon? 97
     Alien Lunar Obelisks? 97
     A Lunar Bridge? 98
     The Tower? 98
     Lunar Domes? 99
     Witnesses? 100
   What About Mars? 101
     Similarities to Earth 101

    An Alien Base on Mars? 102
    Pyramidal Structures 103
    A Space Port? 103
    Egyptian Pyramids and Sphinx in Cydonia? 103
    The Mars Face 104
    A Face in Utopia? 105
    An Underground Base? 106
Earth: The Model Terrestrial Planet 106

Chapter 7: The Intraterrestrials 108
Can Aliens Dig Underground Without Being Discovered? 108
Man-Made Underground Facilities 109
Polar Access Areas? 111
    Richard Byrd's Polar Flights 111
Underwater Entrances or Bases? 112
    The Bermuda Triangle 112
    Japan's Devil's Triangle 114
    The Great Lakes Triangle 114
    More UFOs Sightings Over Water 115
Myths Are Based on Reality 116
    The City of Ur 116
    The Iliad and the Odyssey 117
    The Flood 117
    Atlantis? 118
    Sumerian Myths 120
    African Dogon Myths 120
Myths About Underground Races 122
    Eskimos 122
    Native Americans 122
    The Nagas of India 123
    Agharta 123
    Norse Myths 123
    Nazi German Belief in an Underworld 124
Locations of Underground UFO Bases? 124
    Mount Rainier, Washington? 125
    Mount Lassen, California? 125
    Mount Shasta, California? 125
    Brown Mountain, North Carolina? 126

Chapter 8: Aliens: Their Origin And Links to Mankind 127
Gods or Pilots? 127

Gods From Other Planets? 127
Scientific Proof That Gods Were Aliens? 128
Gods or Demons? 129
Why Did Aliens Come to Earth Originally? 129
Alien Genetic Intervention? 130
The African Connection 132
    Were Africans the First "Chosen People"? 132
    Testimony by The Sphinx? 133
    Other Sculptural Corroboration? 134
Other Evidence of Alien Intervention? 136
    An Old Sparkplug? 137
    Ancient Airplanes? 137
    A Mechanical Starfinder 138
    Electricity in Ancient Times? 139
    Atomic Weapons in The Distant Past? 139
    Testimony by The Palenque Relief? 140
Personal Alien Visits? 141
    To Adolf Hitler? 142
    To Napoleon Bonaparte? 142
    To Charles XII? 143

Chapter 9: The Government's UFO Coverups 144
Passive Coverups 144
The Beginning of Active Coverups 144
    A Review of the Roswell Coverup 144
    The Secret Arctic Operation 145
    Majestic-12 145
    Project Sign 147
    Project Grudge 148
    Project Blue Book 148
    NATO Coverups 149
    Area 51 Revealed 150
Government Sources Confirm The Reality of UFOs 151
    Major Jesse Marcel 151
    Dr. J. Allen Hynek 152
    Robert Dean 152
    Admiral Roscoe Hillenkoetter 153
    Colonel Phillip J. Corso 153
    Astronaut Edgar Mitchell 153
    An Air Force Textbook 154
Does Our Government Have an Agreement With Aliens? 154

Reasons for Government Coverups 155

Chapter 10: How The Truth About UFOs Could Impact Our Lives 158
The Implications 158
   The Intellectual Impact 158
   The Social Impact 159
   The Spiritual/Religious Impact 159
Conclusions 160

Appendices
   A. Men in Black–Real or Hoax? 162
   B. Sample Government Documents 165
   C. UFO Organizations–Where to Report Sightings 171
   D. Glossary 173

Bibliography 179
Credits for Compiled Photos, ... 183
Illustrations and Documents 183

Why I Wrote This Book

Attitudes

I'm sure you remember reading about a time, centuries ago, when we thought the Earth was the center of the universe. We believed this so strongly, in fact, that we automatically rejected any differing views, regardless of how convincing the evidence was. The brilliant mathematical physicist Galileo Galilei died under house arrest in the 17th century for daring to present evidence supporting the Copernican theory of a heliocentric planetary system. Why did we cling so tenaciously to Ptolemy's old geocentric view? For the same reason we cling to so many antiquated views today–fear of attitude adjustment.

Discarding or replacing a view always involves an attitude adjustment, whether it's a minor tweak or a major overhaul. Such adjustments take us out of our attitudinal comfort zones and make us feel insecure until we've integrated the new views into our system. In many cases the implications of the changes are far-reaching and entail adjustments in more than one area of life, making us even more uncomfortable and insecure. For example, changing the view that the Earth was the center of the universe not only necessitated an adjustment of our attitudes about the Earth's relationship to the other known planets, but also about the Earth's role in God's overall scheme of things.

The reality of UFOs is a current example of a concept for which overwhelming proof exists, but which many of us stubbornly refuse to accept for fear of the discomforts of attitude change. We instinctively know that changing our views on UFOs will entail potentially painful adjustments in more than one area of life, as did those who resisted the heliocentric view of our solar system. But, as we all know, accepting the heliocentric view has turned out to be much less painful and infinitely more beneficial than originally anticipated, as will accepting the truth about UFOs. Perpetuating a world view without the reality of UFOs is like perpetuating one without the reality of heliocentricity. There's only so far we can develop using knowledge based on a faulty premise. So, this book is, in part, an attitude check and an invitation to change yours if you haven't already.

Questions and Answers

The other reason why I wrote this book involves questions and answers. First, to answer some of those pressing questions about UFOs that you had already posed but had probably presumed were unanswerable. Second, to raise and answer other equally important questions that may not yet have occurred to you, but likely would have sooner or later. For most answers, I will illustrate my point with pertinent reports on UFO sightings. My intention, however, is not to pretend to have all the answers or to foist exhaustive and preemptive answers on you, for to do so would falsely imply that the truth goes no further than this book. Instead, I intend to satisfy your basic hunger for answers, while deepening your interest and stimulating your appetite for more. Thus, if, by the end of this book, you find that most of your questions about UFOs have been answered, yet you crave more information, then I will have achieved my goal. The list of books in the bibliography would be an excellent aid for continuing your reading on this topic. Now it's time to begin our adventurous journey together. Before we do, however, just a small word of warning: If you've claimed that a lack of answers is the reason why you've resisted the acceptance of UFOs as a reality, you may have to find a different excuse after reading this book!

Chapter I

The Starting Point

What Are UFOs?

Suffice it to say at this point that when I use the term unidentified flying object, I am referring to flying objects of extraterrestrial origin of various shapes and sizes that are based on technology vastly superior to our own. Their colors range from very light to very dark shades. Their sizes vary greatly, ranging, in rare cases, from a few inches in diameter to over twice the size of a football field. Normally the range is somewhere in between. Among the dozens of shapes reported, the most frequent are flat and circular or elliptical, like a saucer (hence *flying saucer*); round, like a ball; oblong, like a cigar; saturn-shaped, like a ball with a horizontal saucer in the middle; and conical (see figures 1 and 2). Some UFOs have even been reported to change their shapes in mid-flight.

Some UFOs are completely silent, while others emit various noises, like roars, booms, whirring, humming, and hissing. Most have no visible discharges as they fly, but some have been reported to emit what seems like fire or vapor from their rear sections. They fly alone and in groups of various sizes. Their flight speed is at times very slow and at times too fast to follow with the naked eye. They exhibit various flight patterns, including hovering, gliding, wobbling, zigzagging in acute-angle turns, rocking like falling leaves, separating from an apparent larger unit into smaller ones and reversing this process by forming a single unit from smaller ones. They are normally seen just occasionally at a given location. But they sometimes appear in *waves*, which are periods of heightened UFO sightings over an extended region and time frame, lasting from a few weeks to a few years, usually with a perceptible peak in reported activity, or in *flaps*, which, on average, are shorter, more localized and more eruptive periods.

UFO pilots are mortal beings of advanced intelligence and extraterrestrial origin. They are sometimes referred to as extraterrestrials (ETs), extraterrestrial biological entities (EBEs) and sometimes as simply aliens. Some have reportedly exhibited strong extrasensory abilities. They vary significantly in appearance, meaning that they likely comprise more than one distinct group (see figures 3-7). Although they're usually described as about four feet tall give or take six inches, they have occasionally been reported as being anywhere from average size to giants. Most are hairless. Their eye color is usually described as very dark, even black. Their skin color is said to vary anywhere from light gray to dark brown. Some have small heads and features, others have lizard-like features, while others have huge heads and large, lidless, wrap-around eyes. So-called "grays" usually have grayish skin, slits for noses and lips and large black insect-like eyes. Although they vary in the way they dress, they are most often seen in one-piece uniforms that are frequently silver-colored. These descriptions are brief distillations of the thousands of UFO sightings on record (see figures 3-7), and will be used as a foundation to build upon in subsequent parts of the book. During this building process you will see UFOs and their occupants become much more than these initial descriptions.

My UFO Encounter

What happened to the four of us on that clear starry summer night in 1967 sent shock waves throughout that entire region of Pennsylvania and forever changed the way we viewed the universe. We had just finished our junior year of high school and had become friends while attending college prep classes at Lincoln University that July. Being impressed by the campus's beautiful rural setting and spacious fields, we had discussed the possibility of camping out when weather conditions permitted. So, on the evening of July 15th, with flashlights on and sleeping bags under arm, we found a suitable spot in the grassy field about two hundred yards behind the men's dormitory. Soon after slipping into our sleeping bags, we began chatting about teenage topics, drinking our sodas, and watching various stellar phenomena unfolding above us, like summer constellations showing their mythological shapes, the pale speckled Moon nearing its first quarter, and occasional meteor swarms shooting by.

We expected the night to continue along in the same serene manner until we fell asleep. But it didn't. About a half hour after we had settled in, the serenity of our night was interrupted by something quite astounding. A group of brightly shining objects suddenly appeared in the middle of the sky. At first they moved along rather slowly, periodically changing formations. At this point we couldn't make out their structure. All we could see were moving white lights. Then, curiously enough, they stopped in mid-air for a short while and then began moving again. That stop-and-start movement surprised us, but didn't cause us to suspect anything out of the ordinary. We reasoned that they were helicopters doing some type of maneuvers.

That theory was quickly dismissed, however, because the objects that we thought were helicopters began moving in ways and at speeds that no helicopter or any other known aircraft could. We all bolted to seated positions, gasped involuntary exclamations, and pinned our eyes to the sky as the objects darted and flashed around the sky so quickly that it became hard to follow them with our eyes! They zigzagged in every imaginable direction like supersonic fireflies, sometimes in formation and sometimes out! By this time, they appeared to have come closer to the ground, for when they slowed or momentarily halted, we could now see circular arrangements of lights either underneath them or around their peripheries. They were definitely saucer-shaped objects! Mesmerizing us for another few minutes, the objects suddenly zipped away simultaneously. One moment they were there, the next they were gone!

At first, we were inclined to keep the incident to ourselves for fear of ridicule. But after debating it for several minutes, we decided to take our story to the local newspaper. Early the next morning, before our first class, we nervously entered the door to the newspaper's staff office, fully aware of the strong possibility that we would be booted out the door as soon as we uttered the word *flying saucer*. But we had to get it off our chests. Besides, we didn't intend to give our real names, so if they didn't believe us, we wouldn't be identified as the fabricators of a tall tale.

So we told them what had happened. Afterwards, the Executive Editor began asking us a lot of questions about our sighting, but he wasn't taking any notes. He sounded like he was fishing for holes in our story, so we expected him to order us to leave at any moment. It was this growing pessimism that set us up for a shock almost as startling as the one we had experienced the night before.

The Editor suddenly grew silent, looked intently at each one of us, drew a deep breath and said, "My wife saw them too."

We were stunned speechless, at first not sure if he was serious or just pulling our leg. But it quickly became obvious that he was dead serious. He proceeded to explain that he had asked us all those questions to compare our sighting with his wife's, and that what we saw matched hers very closely. Her sighting had been in the same general area, but had occurred several weeks earlier. And because there were now corroborating witnesses for her sighting, the newspaper staff agreed to print our story. Our article created such a stir in the region, that it was quickly picked up by three other area papers.

The Questions

As is usually the case with documented UFO sightings, the newspaper articles on our sighting stirred up a lot of excitement over the possible reality of extraterrestrial visitors and, as expected, raised the same burning questions: What were they really? Where did they come from before they appeared over the campus of Lincoln University? Where did they disappear to after they flew away? Why are they here? These have proven to be the most unanswerable of all the questions posed by UFO witnesses. Unanswerable, that is, until now. After several restless years of searching, grappling, and digging, I finally found the

James Edward Gilmer

answers. Serendipitously, solutions to other related puzzles followed. Puzzles such as the nature of man's relationship with extraterrestrials, where these non-human visitors should fit within our spiritual and philosophical systems, and why they may be gods, demons, guardians, or just neighbors. So read on with an open mind and discover not only elusive answers about UFOs, but also an expanded awareness of mankind itself.

Chariots of Gods or Demons?
The Incredible Truth About UFOs and Extraterrestrials

(Artistic depictions of various UFOs based on witness descriptions)

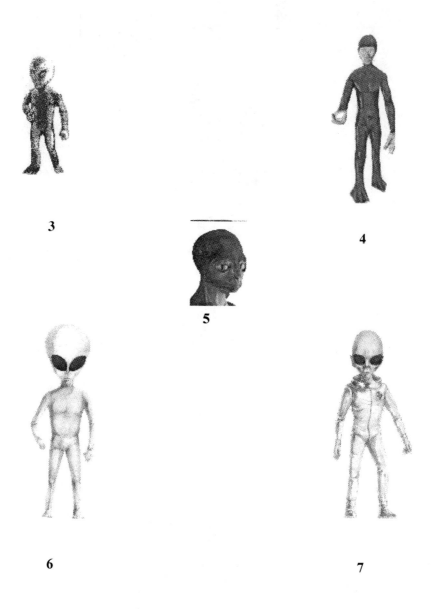

(Artistic examples of extraterrestrial biological entities (EBEs) as described by witnesses)

Chapter 2

About UFO Sightings

Real or Hoax?

Many people scoff at the notion that UFOs are real, believing instead that reports of such sightings are mostly hallucinations, hoaxes, or errors. Although, admittedly, such suspicions have proven to be true in the majority of cases, they should not obscure the fact that literally thousands of other sightings are not hoaxes or errors and defy explanation as anything but a UFO. Take mine, for example. Did the five of us (four students and the Editor's wife) err or hallucinate in an identical manner? We certainly did not conspire to stage a hoax. And what about other even more convincing reports made by well-known and highly credible witnesses? Consider the following three:

An Impeccable Witness: New Hampshire, 1971

It was in the early afternoon under an overcast sky, and Paul and his brother Joseph had just attended the local Memorial Day parade and were on their way to check on some equipment that they had left in an open field on the previous day. Suddenly Joseph slammed on the brakes, causing the truck to skid along the heavily wooded dirt road until it finally came to a halt. For there, floating about three feet off the ground before them was a grayish elliptical object about fifteen feet long described by the two witnesses as shaped "like a squashed pear without a neck." The object abruptly rose into the air, and as it did, the brothers glimpsed horizontal indentations around its entire periphery. It continued to rise, picking up speed as it did, until it soon vanished from sight. After initially deciding not to tell anyone of their unusual experience, the two eventually changed their minds and reported it to the nearby Pease Air Force Base in Portsmouth, New Hampshire. Regarding the credibility of the witnesses, Paul was just about to finish his graduate studies and begin his first assignment as a Roman Catholic Priest! (Fowler, 1974).

A Prominent Witness: Georgia, 1969

On January 6, 1969, at about 7:15 p.m., a well-known gentleman with a degree in nuclear physics was standing outside the local Lions Club in Leary, Georgia, just minutes from entering to deliver a speech. A group of about a dozen men stood there with him. Suddenly their attention was drawn to a bright object hovering silently and motionlessly in the sky above them. This gentleman described it as round, about the size of the Moon, and changing colors from a bluish to a reddish hue. It hovered at a distance of somewhere between 300-1000 yards away and about 30 degrees above the horizon.

The object also seemed to notice the gawking group below, for it glided toward them and then moved away several times. The group watched the object dance back and forth for about another ten minutes before it finally flew away and disappeared. This well-known gentleman filed an official report on the incident in October 1973 at the National Investigations Committee on Aerial Phenomena (NICAP). Oh, by the way, this gentleman with a degree in nuclear physics was former U.S. President Jimmy Carter, who was Governor of Georgia at the time of the sighting and campaigning for his future job at the White House (see figure 8)! (Reader's Digest).

Filing a report of a UFO that he had sighted while governor of Georgia, Jimmy Carter described a round, self-luminous object that first appeared bluish, then turned reddish. The first page of the report is reproduced above.

8

A Trusted Witness: Sweden, 1957

Karin and Ernst Akerberg had just exited their cottage on the evening of August 5, when a mysterious object suddenly flew overhead from the direction of the nearby sea. The couple estimated its altitude at about 200 yards and could see many of the external features of the craft. It was disk-shaped, silvery in color, about 25 yards in diameter, and had seemed to have an upper section that slowly rotated above the lower one. It also emitted a shimmering light around its outer circumference and made a "clicking" noise. After flying past the couple for several more yards, it veered sharply, stopped and hovered, tilted onto its edge and swayed for a while. Then it veered sharply again and flew out of sight. Shortly afterwards, another apparently identical craft flew from the direction of the sea, maneuvered above the amazed couple in a manner almost identical to that of the first one, and then zipped out of sight. They reported the incident to the Swedish Air Force, who investigated and classified it as "unidentified." Incidentally, Ernst Akerberg was an off-duty policeman! (Reader's Digest)

As seen from these sightings, the credibility of some UFO witnesses is virtually unquestioned. And these are just three of many such reports that you will read about in the sections and chapters that follow. Who knows how many more UFOs are sighted by credible witness but remain unreported because the witnesses fear negative repercussions on their reputations and careers?

Close Encounters

Human experiences with UFOs are often classified as various types of *close encounters*. These are close encounters of the first, second, third, and fourth kinds. A person has *close encounter of the first kind* (CE-1) when he or she sights an unidentified flying object at close range; that is, at a distance close enough to make out at least some details of the surface of the object. Just seeing an unidentified object flying at a great distance in the sky does not constitute a close encounter. That would be called a sighting. Of course, all visual perceptions of UFOs are generally called sightings. They become close encounters when the observer is at least close enough to meet the above criteria for a close encounter of the first kind. By this definition, my sighting was a close encounter of the first kind, since we could make out details of the craft's lights in addition to its shape.

A *close encounter of the second kind* (CE-2) occurs when some perceptible evidence of a UFO visit is left behind. Such evidence includes things like holes bored through ice, burned grass and soil, depressions in the ground, burned skin from close proximity to a UFO, and myriad other possibilities.

Some people claim to have seen not only close-up views of UFOs, but also of their occupants. They say they've seen the aliens inside the craft. These people have had a *close encounter of the third kind* (CE-3).

The last of the close encounters is also the most controversial one. A *close encounter of the fourth kind* (CE-4) involves close physical contact with UFO occupants and is most frequently seen in abductions, which we will further discuss a little later.

Since the overwhelming majority of the encounters we will examine during the course of this book are CE-1s and CE-2s, there is no need to focus on them here. CE-3s and CE-4s, however, are relatively rare and merit special attention.

James Edward Gilmer

Close Encounters of the Third Kind

The Wave of 1973

The year 1973 brought not only a wave of general UFO sightings, as we will see in the following chapters, but also a wave of a more specific kind. The third kind, to be exact. The following examples are from that year.

Falkville, Alabama, October 17

Upon initial inspection, Falkville police officer Jeff Greenhaw found no sign of the "spaceship" that a woman had claimed to have seen landing behind her house that evening. Not sure of her seriousness, but willing to give her the benefit of the doubt, he drove around the general area a bit longer. Driving down a nearby road, he spotted what looked like small person about 4 feet tall in a one-piece silver-colored uniform standing a few yards from the road. Startled at first, but concluding that it was just someone wearing a costume as some sort of prank, the officer chuckled, stopped his car and called out, "howdy, stranger!" The figure began walking toward the police cruiser, and the officer, still playing along with the prankster, exited the car and began taking snapshots. As the figure got very close, the officer suddenly realized that it wasn't a *normal* person. He jumped back into his car and turned on the flashing light. Alarmed, the figure began running away. In his haste to catch up with the entity, the officer spun his wheels, kicking up gravel and dust all around him. When the dust had settled, the strange figure had vanished. "It scared me to death," recalled the officer. (Fowler)

Did the woman and the police officer hallucinate about the same sighting? Collaborate on a hoax? Highly unlikely.

Athens, Georgia, October 19

Two nights after the Alabama sighting, another was reported in Athens, Georgia. A resident named Paul Brown, who was driving at the time, spotted an object flying overhead and described it as conical in shape, radiating a bright light and emitting a "swishing sound" as it flew by. Instead of continuing straight ahead, however, the object landed several yards directly in front of the startled Brown. He screeched on his brakes, slid to a stop and watched in petrified horror as two small humanoids exited the craft and began walking toward him! Like the creature that officer Greenhaw spotted (in Alabama), these two were short in stature, about 4 feet tall. They wore identical clothing, a one-piece silver-colored uniform (like the one in Alabama). Regaining his mobility, the panic-stricken Brown reached into his glove compartment and pulled out a pistol to protect

Chariots of Gods or Demons?
The Incredible Truth About UFOs and Extraterrestrials

himself against the approaching pair. As he stepped out of his car and pointed the pistol at them, they turned, hurried back to their ship and lifted off with a "whooshing" sound. (Fowler)

Just a coincidence that two identical sightings occurred two nights apart, both in southern states and involving identical beings?

Hartford City, Indiana, October 22

At about 10:00 that evening, as Mr. and Mrs. Dewayne Donovan were driving along State Road 26, they suddenly spotted two strange-looking humanoid beings moving around in the middle of the road. Mrs. Donovan stopped the car to avoid hitting them. But when she got a good look at them, she put the car in gear, swerved around the beings, and sped away. Again, the humanoids were described as short, about 4 feet tall, and wearing one-piece silver-colored clothing.

The Donovans called the state police from the nearest phone booth and described what they had seen. Responding to the call, Deputy Sheriff Ed Townsend drove to the area to investigate. At first he saw nothing. Driving a little further he stopped to avoid hitting an unusual cluster of animals that was crossing the road at the time. The group consisted of rabbits, cats, a raccoon, an opossum, and possibly others. Simultaneously the officer heard a strange high-pitched noise. Puzzled, Townsend panned his spotlight in the direction that the animals were coming from and that's when he spotted them. Two beings that apparently fit the description of those reported by the Donovans. In addition to their short stature and silver uniforms, they had what appeared to be oval-shaped heads covered by some type of device that resembled a gas mask. Within a few seconds, they rose into the air and disappeared. (Fowler)

It's noteworthy that this sighting occurred so close in time and location to the others. The aliens involved seemed to have a special agenda to be carried out during a limited period of time that year. The next sighting appears to corroborate this.

Goffstown, New Hampshire, November 4

A little after midnight as they lay in bed, Rex and Theresa Snow heard a loud "brushing sound" against their house. Rex rose to investigate, but found nothing, so he went back to bed. Shortly thereafter, the family dog, Miko, began making whining noises in the kitchen. Believing the dog needed to go outside, Rex got up again to let him out. As he reached the kitchen, he noticed a bright light shining in under the shades. The dog was crouched near the door with teeth bared and growling.

When Rex opened the door he expected to find a fire or someone headlights shining toward the house, but a much different spectacle awaited him. Two short humanoids with oval faces wearing one-piece silver uniforms. They appeared to have large ears that rose to a point, dark sunken eyes and a large nose covered by something resembling a hood. The fearful Mr. Rex, ordered the dog to attack them, but it refused. He went and got his pistol, but was too afraid to shoot it at them. His wife soon realized that something was going on downstairs, but she stayed in bed, hoping that it was nothing serious. Meanwhile, the dumbfounded Rex watched in relief as the two figures turned and walked out of sight into the woods. (Fowler)

Again, the similarities among these sightings are difficult to dismiss as mere coincidence. The aliens clearly had some special assignment in the eastern part of the United States during that period of 1973. Why else would they appear so close together? An important fact learned from this last sighting is that some extraterrestrials have large noses and ears in contrast to many reports that describe these features as small or even nonexistent. This reinforces something that I pointed out in Chapter I, namely that extraterrestrials comprise various groups with various external sizes and appearances.

Valensole, France, 1965

The sun had barely risen when Maurice Masse climbed aboard his tractor to work in his lavender field in the Basses Alpes that first day of July. In about an hour, he stopped to have a cigarette. After just a few drags, he heard a peculiar sound behind him. A shrill kind of sound, somewhat like that of a helicopter. As he turned and fixed his eyes on the source of the noise he saw that it wasn't a helicopter. As a matter of fact it wasn't anything that he had ever seen or heard of before. It was about as big as a small car, roughly oval-shaped and grayish in color. Looking underneath it, he noticed six legs stretching out from the center in a circular arrangement and a somewhat thicker pole in the middle protruding straight down into the soil below (see figure 9). His attention was diverted from the object by two small humanoid beings standing nearby. They were bent down towards the ground, apparently occupied with some lavender plants. At first glance, he assumed that they were boys and suspected them of being

9

the culprits who had been vandalizing areas of lavender plants in recent days. But after walking toward them to within about 15 feet, he could see that they were neither boys nor human. He estimated their height at a little over three and a half feet. They had large round heads that were completely bald, huge slanted eyes, a lipless slit for a mouth and grayish skin color. They either didn't have noses or they were so small that Masse couldn't see them from where he stood.

The two humanoids stood up and turned toward Masse. One of them pointed a small pen-like device at him. He didn't feel anything, but noticed that he couldn't move. He stood there, immobile, and watched as they started back to their craft in "falling and rising" motions like "bubbles in a bottle." Their motion was apparently being aided by "bands of light" that were shining on them.

After the beings entered the object, its legs and center pole retracted, then it rose with the same shrill sound that he had heard initially and quickly disappeared through the clouds.

About 15 long minutes after the craft took off, Masse's mobility returned. He raced back home and told his family and friends what had just happened. Then he went to town and reported it to the local gendarmerie. For the next few days, the authorities, private investigators and crowds of visitors visited the UFO landing site and gawked at the impressions made in the soil by the object's legs and at the hole left by the center pole. Soon, Masse, fearful that residue from the craft might have harmful effects on his health, filled the impressions and the hole. Interestingly enough, two years later, Masse took curious UFO investigators there, and they found that the site was still distinguishable from the rest of the landscape, because the lavender plants around its perimeter continually withered prematurely. Finally, weary of all the publicity, Masse ploughed up the lavender plants and converted the area to a wheat field. (Stuttman, vol.16)

It's likely no mere coincidence that this occurred near mountains, as we'll discuss shortly.

The "Socorro Affair", 1964

10

On April 24, as a New Mexico patrolman Lonnie Zamora (figure 10) chased a speeder, he spotten what appeared to be blue flames streaking across the sky towards a dynamite shack on the southern outskirts of the town of Socorro. Needless to say, Zamora abandoned his pursuit of the speeder to investigate the strange aerial phenomenon. After driving to the spot where he thought the object was heading, he got more than a little surprise. The blue flame was now an egg-shaped object resting on the ground atop landing pods. As he got a little closer, his surprise turned quickly to shock when he suddenly saw two small humanoids standing beside the craft. He described the pair as appearing "like a boy or small adult." Their garments were a very light color, like white or beige. When Zamora inched closer for a better look, the beings hastened back into the ship and disappeared in a loud roar. Stunned, Zamora was still lucid enough to phone for help. The police officer who responded found him pale and sweaty, as though he had just experienced some type of trauma. Upon closer inspection of the landing site, they found burned soil and four indentations that matched the landing pods described by Zamora (see figure 11 below)! (Story)

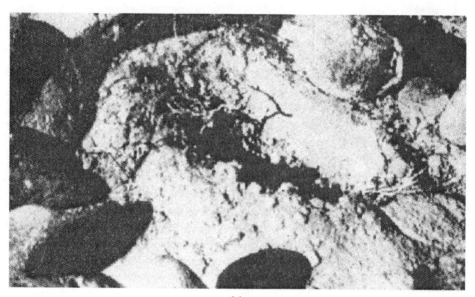

11

(Ground impression left by UFO reportedly seen by Zamora)

The Wilcox Sighting, New York, 1964

Interestingly enough, another virtually identical sighting was reported in the state of New York just a few hours earlier than the Socorro sighting. On the morning of 24 April, at about 10:00, a dairy farmer by the name of Gary T. Wilcox spotted an egg-shaped object in the middle of his field in the town of New Valley. Almost immediately afterwards, two short humanoids emerged from the object wearing very light garments and carrying what looked like trays. He described their clothes as seamless one-piece outfits. They also wore a hood that covered their faces. Suddenly one of them began communicating with

Wilcox in what he perceived as very clear English. The being explained that the trays were to collect soil samples. After fairly lengthy "conversation" the being asked him to bring a bag of fertilizer to that spot and Wilcox agreed. The beings then took off in the craft. Wilcox left, returned with a bag of fertilizer and placed it on the spot where the craft had landed. The next morning when he check, the bag was gone. (Bowen)

Do UFOs Often Leave Solid Evidence of Their Presence?

No question! Although UFOs usually leave without a trace, their presence often causes several different types of lingering effects that many people consider irrefutable proof that they were there, even if they didn't see the UFO itself. Some of these effects are made when the objects land and take off. They leave such things as indentations in the ground (see figure 11) shaped like the spacecrafts' contours and landing gear, as we saw in the last two cases, or scorch marks where prints of the UFO parts that touched the ground are burned into the grass or soil (see figures 12, 13). Indentations and scorchings are two reasons for the so-called *crop circle* images seen in various locations. Other telltale signs of some UFOs that land or fly very close to the ground include thick mist, and vapor trails. Recalling the earlier section on close encounters, you probably know that these signs are examples of *close encounters of the second kind.*

More Ground Depressions – Tennessee, 1973

On the afternoon of September 30, during the UFO wave of 1973-74, a hunter in the dense woods of Lawrenceburg, Tennessee, was perched quietly and motionlessly on a tree branch, eyes fixed on the ground below, awaiting the arrival of an unsuspecting deer. Suddenly he forgot about remaining still, and the hunt became the farthest thing from his mind. His eyes and mind were now riveted on a round, glowing white object that had just flown from an open field into the woods and passed directly in front of him just a few feet away. It appeared to be about ten feet in diameter and was completely silent as it slowly descended on tripodal legs to the ground below, fully visible to the mesmerized hunter. After it landed, a door opened, although the hunter had noticed no lines on the object that would have indicated that it had one. The door swung down to form a ramp, and the hunter fully expected to see something walk down it. Without thinking, he sniffed in response to cold symptoms that were plaguing him. Immediately thereafter, as though the object's occupants had detected him, the door slammed shut, the landing gear was retracted, and the spherical craft zipped up and away at a blinding speed. Climbing down from his perch and inspecting the site of the landing, the hunter noticed a thick mist concentrated directly above the area and three clear depressions in the grass made by the ship's landing gear. (Jacobs, 1975)

More Ground Depressions: Transylvania Alps, Romania, 1972

Late on the evening of September 27, 1972, a night watchman at the parish of Posesti spotted a strange object descending from the sky to a hillside of the nearby Transylvania Alps. He knew it wasn't a conventional aircraft, certainly unlike any he had ever seen. He described the incident to local friends and acquaintances, and was met with strong skepticism because of his advanced age and the fact that it was dark at the time of his sighting. But, they decided to give him a fair chance to prove his story. So, the next morning, they followed him to the spot of the alleged sighting, fully expecting him to have an excuse prepared as to why they could find no evidence. To their surprise, however, they encountered things that they couldn't dismiss. For example, at the spot of the landing, which was in a cornfield, they found a group of corn stalks crushed down to a height of slightly over 3 feet from the ground. Next they noticed that the patch of crushed corn stalks formed a circle about 20 feet in diameter, which was about the shape and size that the watchman had estimated the object to be. Furthermore, three equidistant imprints indented the ground around the circle's perimeter, giving the impression of a circular aircraft that had landed on a tripod!

A team of investigators from Bucharest University came to examine the site and, after meticulous observations and measurements, confirmed that a very massive object had indeed landed on a tripod there. Judging from the height of the bent corn, they concluded that the tripod was about three feet in length. Also, they reported that the soil and vegetation at the site had been scorched and that the soil contained unusual radioactivity. (Ortzen)

Steam and Perforated Ice in Bodies of Water– Cape Cod, 1971

UFOs are also known to travel in large bodies of water and often create physical evidence when they do. For instance, some people have seen huge clouds of steam billow up after UFOs enter the water, because of the hot outer surfaces that some of them apparently have. In extremely cold areas, alien ships are sometimes seen piercing thick ice sheets on their way down into the water underneath, leaving gaping holes in the ice that are often the same shape as the spaceships.

A boy named John had just left home to catch his school bus on the morning of January 7 when he spotted a cigar-shaped object flying out of the clouds towards the ground. He said the object was somewhat larger than an ordinary aircraft and emitted an orange-colored flame from its rear. After the object had descended out of view behind some trees, apparently on its way towards nearby Lake Scargo, the awe-struck John began yelling the only phrase that he knew to describe what he thought he had just seen: "flying saucer!" His frantic screams attracted both his mother and a neighbor, who initially didn't believe his incredible story. But when they followed him to the lake, where he insisted the object went, the two women were stunned to find a large oblong hole in the ice atop the lake, with thick steam rising up from water which was still churning, as if something large, oblong, and hot had just entered it! (Fowler, 1974)

Electrical Disturbances – Brazil, Illinois, 1957

UFOs cause yet another lingering effect that is perhaps the most frequent and the most compelling of all–electrical disturbances! The general belief is that many UFOs emit powerful electromagnetic fields that cause such disturbances. These effects range from instrument panels going haywire to power outages, which are the most common of all. Mogi Mirim, Brazil experienced a blackout in 1957 at the same time as three UFOs were reportedly seen overhead. During the same year, the power went out in Tamaroa, Illinois as a UFO hovered above it.

Other Power Station Outages – Brazil, 1959; New York, 1966

UFOs seem to be drawn to power lines and power stations, where they are often seen hovering or flying above them. As you can probably guess, many of these visits cause power outages. In 1959, according to a news report from Umberlandia, Minais Gerais, Brazil, the automatic keys at a power station there switched off as a circular UFO flew overhead. The keys turned back on after the object had left the area. One of the most famous of all UFO-related blackouts occured in New York in 1966. It is sometimes referred to as the Great Northeast Blackout. It happened as a glowing spherical UFO was seen flying over the power lines of the Niagara Falls power station. Just seconds after witnesses sighted the object, thirty-six million residents lost power in their homes in an area comprising eighty thousand square miles! (Fowler, 1974)

James Edward Gilmer

12

13

(1971 photos of impressions burned into the grass and soil near Lignon, France)

Chariots of Gods or Demons?
The Incredible Truth About UFOs and Extraterrestrials

Are UFOs Seen Mostly in America?

Not at all. As you read further, you will see that UFO sightings are a truly international phenomenon. Every culture ever known to man, regardless of how advanced or primitive, has reported encounters with UFOs. And the stark similarities in the descriptions of UFOs from all parts of the world have been much too consistent to dismiss as mere coincidence.

Are UFO Sightings Strictly a Modern Phenomenon?

The *modern* era of UFO sightings is generally said to have begun on 24 June 1947, when a Boise, Idaho, businessman and air rescue pilot named Kenneth Arnold, on his way to help find a missing plane, spotted nine disk-shaped objects over Mount Rainier, Washington, that were flying like "saucers skipping over water (see figure 14)." Although Arnold popularized the term, *flying saucer* he wasn't the first on record to use it.

That honor belongs to a Texas farmer named John Martin, who, on January 24, 1878, saw unidentified objects flying above him and described them as "saucers."

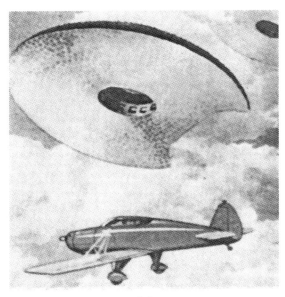

14

(Cover of Arnold's Book *Coming of the Saucers*)

Now, back to the beginning of the modern era. While I agree that the Arnold sightings most likely triggered the media attention that led to the global popularity of UFOs and to their status as fixtures in our imagination, I disagree that the modern era began in 1947. Judging from a host of documented sightings and reliable witnesses, I think it more accurate to say that the modern era actually began in the middle of World War II, and I'll show you why in Chapter 4.

So, what I'm saying is that UFO sightings began in 1878 and became a modern phenomenon during World War II, right? Wrong! Most hoax/error theorists probably wish they could say UFO sightings began that recently, so they could strengthen the argument that UFOs are just figments of our modern imagination. But they can't. Evidence of UFO sightings goes back even farther than the written records of our earliest civilizations! Those of you who have read such authors as Peter Kolosimo and Erich von Daeniken are aware of this. In subsequent chapters of this book I will take you back to a few of those ancient sightings within the context of some of the questions that I address.

Chapter 3

Why Have Aliens Been Visiting Us?

After doing the math, the answers appear almost ridiculously obvious to me, and hopefully they will to you, too. UFOs have been visiting us for two very clear reasons. Reasons which have their roots far back in our past. After I state the reasons, we will explore them and their roots more deeply as the book progresses. First, however, I'll offer you the opportunity to weigh some of the evidence (sightings) and reach your own conclusions. But please don't interpret this as a guessing game. My expectation is that the reasons that I present for extraterrestrial visitations will be far more convincing after you discover them yourself then find out that your conclusions match my own. Beforehand, I'll briefly alert you to three very important patterns in UFO appearances that you need to bear in mind while reviewing the sightings.

Patterns

Three significant patterns have become evident regarding the behavior of UFOs. They involve where UFOs are most likely to be sighted. While it's true that UFOs are spotted flying and hovering over every imaginable place in the world, be it cities, farms, highways or dirt roads, they are sighted with disproportionate frequency in the following locations: 1) in certain geographic regions, 2) near power stations and man-made aircraft, and 3) in places of conflicts and threats.

Geographic Areas

Although some people are aware that UFOs are seen with unusual frequency near certain geographic areas, including mountains and valleys, forests, polar regions, and large bodies of water, they are not sure whether these appearances are a matter of simple coincidence or whether a discernible pattern is involved. My own research has led me to the conclusion that there is a definite pattern, meaning basically that UFOs appear more in those areas than others intentionally and for definite reasons. This pattern and the reasons behind it help form the basis of my answer to another important question that we will discuss in a subsequent chapter; namely, where UFOs go when they disappear from sight. I wanted to bring these types of sightings to your attention in this chapter, because you will encounter them in many of the sightings reports that I present, long before we reach the chapter on where UFOs go. By sensitizing you to their appearance now, you will thus be more receptive when I address them within the context of where UFOs go following a sighting.

Power Stations and Man-Made Aircraft

UFOs are frequently spotted near power stations (nuclear and regular) and man-made aircraft. You've already seen examples of sightings near power stations. In the sections to come, you will see more of these as well as several examples of UFOs chasing and pacing man-made aircraft. This type of UFO behavior hints strongly at one of the reasons for their visitations. Consider the following sighting near a man-made aircraft.

Space Shuttle Columbia, Cape Canaveral 1996

On the night of February 25, a CNN camera man had his equipment pointed upward, filming the broken end of a 12-mile tether hanging from the shuttle that had broken during a failed attempt to haul a satellite into position. Little did he know that his camera would capture the image of something far more significant than either the shuttle or the broken tether. Within seconds, a strange object streaked into the camera's field of view. It was light yellow and shaped like a spinning top. Another person carrying a video camera also filmed it. After just a few minutes of moving slowly past the shuttle, the object darted away out of sight. The most obvious assumption, of course, is that the UFO was there because of the shuttle. If so, why? Hold that question until after the following section on conflicts and threats. At that point, you will very probably have named the reasons for UFO visitations. If not, I'll tell you.

Places of Conflicts and Threats

This pattern is more reflective of why UFOs visit us is than is any other pattern. As a matter of fact, in my opinion, this is the most frequent, the most evident and the most convincing pattern of all, which is why I saved it for last. It is so transparent in its message, in fact, that just knowing what the pattern is will very likely bring the *aha* reaction to your lips before you even read the sightings reports. It includes some of both reasons for UFO visitations. Stated in a bit more detail, this pattern is one in which UFOs are seen most frequently in times and areas of military conflicts and near military and other areas where equipment and conditions exist that potentially threaten the safety of human life and/or the environment. In other words, UFOs appear most often in places and times of perceived conflicts and threats. What proof do I have for this pattern? Documented sightings, of course. Literally thousands of them. It is not my intention, however, to dilute my point by inundating you with sightings, so let's review just a few of them. If you haven't already blurted out the two reasons for UFO visitations, you soon will.

Afghanistan and Pakistan, Fall, 2001; August, 2000

These regions are rife with military conflicts and threats. Pakistan, of course, is a newcomer in the nuclear arms club and recently tested its atomic weapons. In the Fall of 2001, during the U.S.- led bombing of the Taliban in Afghanistan, there were unsubstantiated reports of unidentified objects flying and hovering near the areas of conflict. My efforts to corroborate them with reliable eyewitness accounts and/or solid documentary evidence have thus far proved fruitless, although I'm still trying. During August of the previous year, however, both reliable eyewitnesses and documentary evidence told of numerous UFO sightings in that area. On the evening of August 24, for example, eyewitnesses in various provinces of Afghanistan, including Kandahar, spotted several bright cylindrical objects in the sky. They moved from Afghanistan, then crossed over into the border towns of neighboring Pakistan. They were seen by high-ranking officials of both countries. In Pakistan, by Colonel Asmatullah, who is chief of military security for the governor of the province of Baluchistan. In Afghanistan, by representatives of the ruling Taliban party.

The Taliban first suspected the objects to be another American cruise missile attack on the hideouts of terrorist multi-millionaire Osama bin-Laden. After checking through radio and satellite communications, however, they quickly learned that the objects not only were not missiles, but were unlike anything else that they were familiar with. They were unidentified flying objects. The Pakistani Airforce was also baffled and sent several reconnaissance planes and helicopters in search of the mysterious objects, but could not catch up with them. (UFO Roundup)

Ashland, Maine, 1999

On June 27, an unidentified flying object was spotted flying toward the center of Ashland. According to witnesses there, it was flying fast at first, but slowed down as it approached. Gawkers below described it as triangular in shape with seven lights around its periphery–all blue. It hovered overhead for a short while, darted away out of sight, then zipped back to the same spot. It repeated these motions several times until it disappeared for good. Interestingly enough, onlookers observed that when the object flew away at a high rate of speed, the blue lights turned red.

Two of the three patterns are involved here. First, Ashland is near a military installation—Loring Air Force Base. Second there are large bodies of water in the area, Squa Pan Lake and the extensive coastal areas of Maine. Did the UFO just happen to be in an area with these military and geographic features? (UFO Roundup, 1999)

Operation Desert Fox, December 1998

This happened during the last year of an international UFO wave that began in 1996. To refresh your memory, Desert Fox was a four-day military operation undertaken by the USA (aided by the Royal Air Force), in which strikes were carried out against military and security targets in Iraq suspected of contributing to the production and storage of weapons of mass destruction. True to their pattern, UFOs began appearing in the areas involved in the conflict. In the pre-dawn hours of December 16, a number of UFOs were seen flying over Baghdad and were described as "V-shaped" and "triangular" in appearance. The objects were filmed by a CNN night-vision camera and aired live on American television. Many witnesses in Baghdad wondered whether the objects were part of the U.S. weaponry being used against targets in their country. At about the same time in the USA, several triangular UFOs were spotted flying over Fort Drum in upstate New York. Fort Drum was a staging area for Desert Fox. A battalion of light infantry troops, in addition to military hardware, was sent to Iraq from Fort Drum.

Actually the first UFO sightings near Fort Drum had begun about two and a half weeks earlier, on November 30. Witnesses said several of the objects had first appeared in the area of Evan Mills, N.Y. and Perch Lake, just west of Fort Drum. One witness said that the unidentified vessels displayed a "large bluish light with a small red streak at its center." Another witness saw the objects move out over the lake before disappearing. (UFO Roundup, 1998)

At this point, let me remind you of the geographic patterns of UFO sightings that I asked you to be aware of. In this one, UFOs are seen over a lake before disappearing. Mere coincidence? And what about the circumstantial pattern? Can it be coincidence that the abovementioned UFOs appeared simultaneously in an area of conflict (Iraq) and an involved military installation (Fort Drum)?

Nellis Air Force Base, Nevada, May 1997

Shortly before noon on May 26, radio host Art Bell and his wife got the surprise of their lives after stepping outside their house to close a fence. His wife,

Ramona, was the first to notice it. Glancing up at the sky, Art spotted a jet plane moving at an unusually high rate of speed, and he pointed it out to Ramona. After getting the binoculars, she peered up at the jet, but saw something else that neither of them had anticipated. Startled, and unable to fully grasp what she saw, she handed the binoculars to Art to get his opinion. What he confirmed was a "cylindrical round object" that glowed "like a hundred watt bulb." It was somewhat larger than the jet and had a bright silvery hue. When he first observed it, it was pacing the jet. Moments later, it abruptly stopped and hung completely motionless in the sky, defying the laws of inertia and gravity. No slowing, no drifting, it just "stopped dead cold" and remained that way for several minutes. During that time, the only movement of any kind by the object was a slight pendulum-like swing (recall the rocking like falling leaves motion described in chapter 1). Then, as suddenly as it had stopped, the object took off "like a bat out of hell" in a steep climb southward and quickly disappeared. After the two related their incident on Art's radio show, several listeners called in to tell the couple that they had seen the same thing. Among the callers was a local deputy sheriff.

This is a classic sighting with several signature UFO elements. It's shape, it's color and brightness, its unusual speed and maneuverability, its rocking motion. Also, in addition to occurring near a military base, it was interacting with a man-made aircraft. The jet pilot was undoubtedly flying as fast as he could to try to escape the UFO. But of course the jet's speed was still compared to the object's, clearly seen by how quickly the object flew out of sight. (UFO Roundup,1997)

Now, what was the object doing near Nellis AFB? Why was it pacing the jet plane? It knew that the pilot was aware of it, so it obviously wasn't trying to stay out of sight. So what was the UFO doing? And why? The answers will become clear very shortly.

Ecuadorian Military Base, June 1996

The naval base and air academy at Salinas, Ecuador, located on the Pacific coast, was shaken from its perfunctory routine one clear afternoon in mid-June. As the base personnel outside were going about their regular duties, they suddenly began halting in their tracks and fixing awed gazes at a point in the sky almost directly above them. What commanded their attention was an unidentified bright, round, object, suspended among the clouds at an estimated altitude of 1000 feet. It hung there for a full two hours after it was spotted. Everybody on base eventually got a look at it, even the base commander, Lt. Colonel Jorge Cabezas Quiroz. Many of the personnel below were alert enough to get their cameras and take snapshots of the object. Finally, the UFO accelerated quickly out of sight. (UFO Roundup,1996)

The two main patterns in this sighting should be easy to identify. First, the UFO is sighted over a military base. Second, there is a large body of water nearby. Mere coincidences? Why did the UFO hover directly above the base for two hours? Were the occupants allowing the craft to cool down after a long day's flight? Were they posing for the cameras below?

Israeli Flap of 1996

Although Israel has been a continuous hotbed of UFO activity since the beginning of recorded history, 1996 was hotter than most recent years, meaning that Israel experienced a flap. What, you might ask, qualified Israel to be included under places of conflicts and threats? Need I go back to the very beginning of Israel's still-unresolved, on-again, off-again struggle with its Arab neighbors? No, I think the Israeli War of Independence (1948) goes far back enough to make my point. Starting in that year, Israel has fought four wars against the Arabs. As a matter of fact, though not openly, Syria is still officially in a state of war with Israel and is one of the enemy states that sponsors ongoing guerilla and terrorist activity against Israel. That coupled with violent Palestinian uprisings called *intifadas*, make this area of the Middle East far from free of conflicts and threats. Predictably, UFO sightings increased during each of the wars.

During the six-day war of 1967, according to various public documents, including Israeli newspapers, superior numbers of enemy soldiers inexplicably abandoned virtually unused armaments and fled before smaller units of Israelis. Also enemy pilots suddenly veered from their targets and took off back to their home bases. Why? According to reported statements by Arab soldiers after the war, strange objects had appeared before them in the skies and unearthly beings on the battlefields, both of which they interpreted as divine in origin. And they dared not fight against divinity. Were the objects in the skies UFOs? Were the strange beings on the battlefields aliens?

At the height of the 1996 flap, on August 4, phones at the police station in Eilat suddenly began ringing off the hook. Excited residents were calling in to report three mysterious balls of bright light in the night sky. One was larger than the other two, and they all intermittently flashed alternating colors. The glittering objects lingered for about thirty minutes then darted away out of sight. A similar sighting occurred three days earlier when a "round reflective object" was seen flying above the skies of Moshav Tomar, in the Jordan River Valley. Two days prior to that, on July 29, bright round objects similar to the ones described above were sighted over Tel Aviv. These objects also emitted alternating colors, mainly blue, green and red.

On September 17, the traffic in Tel Aviv suddenly came to a screeching halt as drivers began stopping their cars and jumping out with eyes and fingers pointed skyward. What the awe-struck spectators saw during the wee hours of that morning was a strange "light-emitting UFO" alternately hovering and flying in loops above them. After about an hour of "doing tricks" the object headed east and disappeared from view. The Israeli newspaper, the *Maariv*, reported the incident and included several Tel Aviv policemen as witnesses.

On September 25, the *Maariv*, reported another sighting, one that had occurred earlier that very morning. Hundreds of Bedouin Arabs witnessed an egg-shaped UFO hovering over the village of Nugidat, near Nazareth. It "emitted blue and violet rays and illuminated a small hill behind the mosque," related a local resident. The object lingered for about four hours, moving slowly along in the sky, and then disappeared. Nazareth's police chief verified the report stating that he, too, had witnessed the UFO. (UFO Roundup, 1996)

These were only a fraction of the total number of sightings during this flap. In addition to occurring in an area of conflict and threat, this flap also occurred near two large bodies of water: the Mediterranean Sea and the Jordan River. Coincidence?

The Belgian Flap of 1989-90

This Belgian flap was part of a larger two-year European wave. The area frequented the most by UFOs during this period was the French-speaking region of Wallonia. Many of these sightings were reported by numerous well-known publications, including the Wall Street Journal. It began in early November, 1989, when thousands of people, including policemen, began witnessing an almost continuous parade of triangular-shaped objects flying overhead in various patterns. Sometimes they would glide slowly along in a straight line. At other times they would execute quick sharp-angle maneuvers that would be impossible for man-made aircraft. Once in a while they would just hover motionlessly above rooftops. The UFOs reportedly had three large bright lights, which the objects seemed to direct towards the ground like search lights. On several occasions, the lights on the craft were reported to change alternately to various colors.

There are a number of military-related installations in the general area of Wallonia, including a Belgian airbase and military radar station. A little farther away in Brussels is a NATO military base and radar station. It was from the latter radar station in Glons that F-16 fighters were ordered to scramble in pursuit of the alien visitors. The jets were able to establish radar contact with the UFOs but could not gain on them. The pilots reported that everytime they got a radar lock on the objects, they seemed to alter their flight patterns, as though they detected the radar. Another interesting fact about NATO involvement during this flap is that NATO had been testing secret military aircraft at the time. (ParaNet, 1991)

Did a UFO flap just happen to occur in a region that hosted Belgian and NATO military installations? Was the fact that secret aircraft were being tested by NATO in the same area also a coincidence?

Fort Benning, Georgia, 1977

John T. Vasquez was a sargeant stationed at Fort Benning, Georgia on September 2, 1977. It is a date indelibly imprinted on his memory. A date on which reality as he knew it changed forever, because what he saw redefined reality. That night, as the 1st battalion assembled outdoors for a meeting among base commanders, Vasquez spotted a mysterious object hovering overhead. It was spherical and bright, noiseless, and unlike anything he had seen thus far in the several years that he had served in the military. He tried to categorize it as something man-made, but he couldn't. Within moments, the object zipped silently away, leaving Vasquez groping for answers. But he wasn't the only witness left stunned by the object. Most of Alpha, Bravo, Charlie, and Delta companies saw it, too. Vasquez began reading books and reports on UFOs and became convinced that what he saw was of extraterrestrial origin, so he embarked on a quest to obtain documents on the incident through the Freedom of Information Act (FOIA). Unfortunately Vasquez has been repeatedly denied access to such documents, and several of the commanding officers present at the time of the incident have since refused to acknowledge it. (CNI News, 2000)

As far as the patterns are concerned, there is, of course, the military base. A geographic pattern is also present. Whether by design or accident, Fort Benning is situated near a large body of water, the Chattahoochee River. Why was the UFO was hovering there? What was it doing? Was it hanging motionless above a military base to rest it's power source?

Iran, 1976

This sighting, which occurred during the wave of 1975-76, involved a UFO that was chased by Iranian jet fighters. The details were provided by the October 1 issue of the Iran Times from taped messages sent by Lieutenant Jafari, one of the Iranian pilots. The UFO was seen near Shahrokhi Air Base in Hamadan, on September 19, and Jafari was sent to investigate it. After he spotted it, he reported that the object, "was about half the size of the Moon as seen from earth." It was "radiating violet, orange, and white light about three times as strong as moonlight." It was already going faster than the speed of sound, and sped up even more when Jafari flew toward it. Even at maximum jet speed, he couldn't keep up with it, as it sped toward Teheran. Jafari was instructed to return to base if he couldn't catch the object, and he agreed. But seconds later, he reported that the object had doubled back and was now pursuing him: "Something is coming at me from behind. It is 15 miles away...now 10 miles...now 5 miles...I think it is going to crash into me! It has just passed by, missing me narrowly." Jafari's voice clearly sounded bothered, and he requested directions back to the base.

Jafari flew back to the base and was replaced by another pilot. The second pilot soon sighted the object and radioed that it had slowed down and that he had just seen "a bright round object with a circumference of about 4.5 meters, leave the UFO." It appeared to be a probe of some type. The object seemed to inspect the jet plane of the second pilot for a brief period, then rejoined the larger craft, which then flew away at what he described as many times the speed of sound.

The reports of the two pilots were further corroborated by several control tower officials at Mehrabad airport and by civilians in the area who called in descriptions that were nearly identical to those of the pilots. (Fawcett, 1984)

Fort Ritchie, Maryland, 1976

On July 30, several witnesses reported seeing three UFOs flying slowly over Fort Ritchie, moving from east to west. They viewed the objects for more than two hours from a number of clear vantage points atop the Catoctin Mountains and described them as being oblong-shaped, about two and a half times the size of a truck, and having a reddish tint. The desk sergeant on duty at the time heard the reports coming in and went to one of the mountaintop sites to investigate. There he observed one of the objects hovering about 150 yards above the ammunition storage area. His report was confirmed by an army police sergeant who was nearby at the time. (Fawcett and Greenwood, 1984)

Fort Ritchie, which is also known as "Site R" is one of the more significant places for UFO sightings, because it combines a number of *signature* UFO elements. First of all, as mentioned above, it is situation in the Catoctin Mountains. Mountains, as pointed out earlier, are one of the geographic areas where UFOs are frequently seen. Secondly, Site R is the home of an extensive underground government facility. UFOs are extensively involved with underground facilities, as we will review a little later in this book. (Sauder, 1995)

Cannon Air Force Base, New Mexico, 1976

The Air Force Operations Center at Cannon AFB reported that two UFOs were observed flying over the base at shortly before 6:00 a.m. on January 21. The witnesses were security police, who described them as disk shaped and about twenty five yards in diameter. The objects glowed with possibly a silvery hue and had a blue light on top. (Fawcett)

That this sighting occurred at any military installation would be sufficient to make my point. But I think it noteworthy to mention that sightings practically anywhere in New Mexico have special significance, because of the history of UFO sightings in that state and the various types of military installations there. We will examine both in more detail further below.

Falconbridge Air Force Station, Ontario, Canada, 1975

This information was obtained from official North American Aerospace Defense Command (NORAD) logs released to a UFO researcher who had requested them under FOIA. The extensive list of sightings in the log indicated that Canada, too, had been very preoccupied with UFO visits. Both the United States and Canada were involved in these particular sightings, apparently due to the fact that Falconbridge virtually straddles the two countries:

From November 12th through the 15th, Falconbridge reported to NORAD the almost constant parade of unusual objects flying overhead. Many of the UFOs were clearly visible on radar and were logged as such. The sightings were confirmed by dozens of witnesses on base plus members of the Ontario Provincial Police. Some of the objects emitted pulsing lights that faded off and on and flew rather slowly and in a jerky manner before they zipped out of sight. The lights on some others appeared more steady and yellowish and their motion was more forward and backward. Still others had distinctly oval shapes and yellow flashing lights. Both Canadian and American jet fighters were deployed to pursue the objects, but could not intercept them. (Fawcett and Greenwood, 1984)

Another reason I chose to point out the Falconbridge sightings is that they share the same special significance that Fort Ritchie does; namely, that this area includes an extensive underground military facility. This is a NORAD facility and is located at North Bay, Ontario. We will cover this in subsequent chapters. (Sauder, 1995)

Loring Air Force Base, Maine, 1975

Loring AFB is home to a munitions storage area where nuclear weapons are stored in huts camouflaged in blankets of dirt to render them invisible to aircraft passing overhead. As one would expect, the half-mile long area is fenced in and tightly guarded 24/7 by military police assisted by K-9 dogs and patrol vehicles. The staff sergeant on duty at the time spotted an unidentified aircraft flying approximately three hundred feet above them. He reported the sighting to the Command Post 42nd Bomb Wing, characterizing it as a penetration of the base by an unknown aircraft. A staff sergeant in the control tower watched the object on the radar screen and confirmed its unknown status. Soon, several other witness had seen the object and the commander of the 42nd Bomb Wing had implemented an alert level of Security Option 3, which was a major-level alert. The object had a white strobe light as well as a reddish or orange light in front that appeared to be used for navigation. It flew rather slowly, at times hovering, then continuing. It was also estimated to be about the size of a helicopter.

The object's size and flight movements led observers to initially conclude that it was a helicopter that had somehow strayed off course. This assessment was soon dismissed, however, because the members of a B-52 bomber crew working out of a launch truck got a clear look at the craft and quickly learned that it was no helicopter. As it hovered in mid-air above them, they could see that it had the shape of a "stretched-out football." As the mesmerized crew continued to gape, the object extinguished its lights and vanished from sight. Soon it reappeared, first moving in a jerky fashion, then hovering silently and motionless. The crew climbed into the truck and drove toward the object trying to get a better look at it. It flew slowly enough for them to finally close to within about three hundred feet of it. At this point it was floating quietly no more than about five feet above the ground, and revealed a lot more detail. It was solid and appeared to have no doors, windows, or engine propellers. Several colors seem to blend together on the object. Soon it shut off its lights and vanished. (Fawcett)

Needless to say, priority reports of this sighting were sent to high-level officials at several government agencies in Washington, D.C. From my perspective, this is another of those incidents with special significance, due to the geographic location of Loring. Naturally it involves water, given the extensive coastal areas in the state of Maine.

Vandenburg Air Force Base, California, 1974

This sighting involved UFOs referred to as "ghost ships" that chased missiles launched toward the Kwajalein test range. The U.S. has been testing its ballistic missile defense system in the Kwajalein Atoll region of the U.S.-held Marshall Island Trust Territory since 1959. In August, 1974, during the UFO wave of 1973-74, the Air Force launched a Minuteman Intercontinental ballistic missile (ICBM) from Vandenburg AFB toward the test range. As is normal procedure, radar operators tracked the progress of the projectile as it flew toward its target. Suddenly, the operators' attention was diverted from the missiles to something else on the radar screens. Something inexplicable and astounding. There, in plain view of the stunned radar experts were unidentified objects flying right next to the nose cone of the ICBM! According to the radar, the UFO was shaped like an inverted saucer and was flying just above the missile to the right. The witnesses gawked at the radar screen as they watched the object cross in front of the missile then drop slightly to a point just below and to the left of the warhead, as though inspecting it! (Fawcett)

Mansfield, Ohio, 1973

This is one of the more remarkable and perplexing sightings on record. It involved a near mid-air collision between a military aircraft and an unidentified flying object that had been chasing it. During a late-night flight on October 18th, the four crew members of an Army helicopter piloted by Captain Larry Coyne noticed a bright red light that suddenly appeared in the eastern sky. At first it seemed to be pacing the helicopter on a parallel course. It abruptly changed course and headed straight toward the helicopter at an estimated six hundred knots. After quickly alerting his crew that the object was on a collision course with them, the alarmed Coyne directed the helicopter into an evasive dive. Amazingly, the object kept pace with the descending helicopter. At that point, the crew got a clear look at it, describing it as an oblong object about fifty to sixty feet long, with a bright red light along the front edge and a green light along the rear underside. The surface of the craft was a gray metallic color which was clearly visible in contrast to the front and rear lights.

Desperate to escape the object, Coyne set the controls for an even steeper and faster descent that estimated at about two thousand feet per minute. Abruptly, the UFO stopped dead in mid-flight, hovered, as if observing the plunging helicopter, and emitted a bright green beam from the lights on the rear underside. Astonishingly, the crew quickly discovered that, instead of descending, they were actually climbing at a speed of one thousand feet per minute! They went rapidly from about 1700 feet to an altitude of above 3700 feet high very rapidly. The UFO, apparently out of concern for the crew's safety, had reversed the direction of the helicopter! "We were supposed to be going down, but we were going up!" exclaimed Coyne. The object quickly accelerated west and disappeared.

Some researchers, trying to explain how the direction of the helicopter could be reversed, have theorized that the UFO must have created some type of anti-gravity vortex around it. Who knows for sure? Again, this is one of the more perplexing sightings on record. Coyne subsequently became part of a delegation to the United Nations encouraging more worldwide attention to the UFO phenomenon (World Almanac, 1981).

Vietnam, 1968

The UFO wave period of 1964-68 offers some clearly unique reports. Among them, the following report of UFOs being sighted and shot at.

Starting in late June 1968, American soldiers stationed at radar outposts south of the demilitarized zone between North and South Vietnam began sighting and reporting almost continuous streams of unidentified objects flying from one side of the zone to the other. The South Vietnamese became quickly aware of them also, and chose to officially describe them as "communist helicopters" that they had been shooting down. These statements, however, were designed for public consumption to quell any possible panic. The truth was that the South Vietnamese government had no idea what the objects invading its skies were, and, while they did shoot at them, they never registered a hit.

A reliable witness to the unidentified nature of the objects was a well-known *Newsweek* reporter by the name of Robert Stokes, who was covering the war and who happened to be present when the UFO reports first began coming in. Among the incidents reported by Stokes, a notable one occurred one evening at about 11:00 p.m. A soldier was observing several of the objects at that time through an electronic telescope and had begun radioing in his account of them. He described them as "thirteen sets of yellowish-white lights" moving west at an altitude of five hundred to one thousand feet above the Ben Hai River. This was corroborated by radar unit Alpha 2. A tracker in this unit exclaimed that he was "surrounded by blips" on his screen. No known aircraft was supposed to be in the area at the time.

U.S. jet fighters were deployed at about 1:00 a.m. to intercept the unauthorized visitors. They shot missiles at the objects and initially thought they had hit one, because one of the missiles exploded in the area of one of the objects. But, as it turned out, they hit nothing. The objects quickly accelerated and disappeared. (Fawcett)

Incidentally, this case contains more than one signature UFO element. First, military involvement. Second, they're flying over a large body of water. Another coincidence?

Ellsworth Air Force Base, South Dakota, 1966

Another clear case of a UFO pursuing and inspecting military hardware. It was in the fall of 1966, in the middle of a smaller UFO wave that lasted from 1965 to about 1967. A crew of five Air Force personnel had just taken off from Ellsworth AFB in a helicopter, en route to a Launch Control Facility located a few miles away. A little more than halfway into the flight, an unidentified object suddenly appeared to the right of the helicopter. It flew on a parallel course at a speed perfectly matching the helicopter's at a steady distance of about 300 feet. It was clearly visible to the entire crew and described as about fifty to sixty feet long, circular with a "cupped upper structure," very bright, and light grey in color. The transfixed crew watched as the object suddenly accelerated from the right side to the front of the helicopter keeping the same distance away. After hovering in that position for a few more seconds, it flew back around to the right side, and zipped away out of sight. (Fawcett)

There are a number of familiar circumstantial facts about this one. First, the UFO was clearly inspecting the military aircraft. Second, it just so happens that Ellsworth AFB is just a stone's throw from the Black Hills, where Mount Rushmore is situated. Third, Black Hills National Park (forest area) is in the general region. All coincidences?

Edwards Air Force Base, California, 1965

What happened on October 7, 1965, at Edwards Air Force Base was so secret that for several years personnel there refused to even acknowledge to the outside world that anything had happened and referred to it amongst themselves as simply "the incident." That night Edwards went on military alert. But it was far from an ordinary alert. It was a UFO alert. Edwards is a highly secure air base, a 301,000 acre facility where astronauts are trained and new classified military aircraft are tested. It's a cause for alarm anytime just one unauthorized conventional aircraft intrudes into its airspace, so it's understandable that there was near panic during the incursion of several unauthorized and unidentifiable aircraft. At about 01:30 a.m., twelve such objects suddenly appeared over the base and were immediately spotted by personnel on the ground. The vessels were simultaneously picked up on base radar screens. The sighting lasted at least five hours, so eyewitnesses on base got a good look at them. Other witnesses from as far away as fifty miles claimed to see them. They danced and hovered at an altitude of about 5000 feet above the runway and didn't appear to be in any discernible formation, except for three of them, which appeared to form a kind of "inverted triangle." The exact shape of the vehicles was hard to make out because of the brightness of their green, white, and red flashing lights and the darkness.

After hours of observing the objects and debating what to do about them, an F-106 interceptor jet was sent up in pursuit at about 05:00 that morning. By then the objects had ascended to about 40,000 feet. As the jet tried to approach them, they accelerated away at speeds that only made the pilot shake his head. Nothing man-made could travel that fast. The air controller at the time, Chuck Sorrels, had directed the jet pilot to the location of the objects and had carried on radio communications with him during the entire chase. The radio talk, which included descriptions of the UFOs were recorded on tape and classified. Sorrels, now retired, recently came forward and acknowledged the reality of the sighting and the chase. What were the UFOs doing at a military test site?

Exeter, New Hampshire, 1965

This is a very high-profile case that attracted nationwide attention and formed the basis of a number of newspaper and magazine articles as well as the national best seller *Incident at Exeter*. At about 1:00 a.m. on September 3, A young man by the name of Norman Muscarello, had tried to hitchhike his way to his home in Exeter from a location about twelve miles away. Due to the sparse traffic at that time of night, he found himself walking most of the way. After about an hour he reached the town of Kensington, and that's where it happened. Something at least the size of a house came flying toward him from the direction of a nearby open field. He described it as about eighty to ninety feet in diameter, with bright red pulsating lights around what appeared to be a front rim on the object. The lights seemed to fade from left to right and then brighten again in a continuous cycle. It's flight motion was a partial wobbling and rocking motion at times, then zigzagging, darting motions in which it would make instant turns at acute angles. All the while, it was completely silent.

After getting a ride into Exeter, Muscarello rushed very excitedly into a police station and began relating his story. He knew how crazy he must have sounded while recapping his experience, but he pleaded with them to believe him. Acting on the young man's obvious sincerity, Officer Toland radioed a patrolman still out on duty for any word he might have heard on any strange sightings that night. To their surprise, that patrolman, Eugene Bertrand, entered the station within five minutes with an odd look on his face and an odd story to tell.

Several minutes before Bertrand was radioed about possible sightings, he had stopped to assist a woman parked by the side of the road near an overpass with a dazed look on her face. After gathering herself a bit, she nervously proceeded to tell Betrand about a strange silent object that had swooped down out of the sky and pursued her for about twelve miles, breaking off the chase as she reached the overpass. After she had finished describing the object's appearance, Bertrand politely bade her goodbye, not even bothering to report the incident because he "thought she was a kook." But after being radioed from the station about a possible sighting, Bertrand came in to relay the woman's story, suspecting that he might have been wrong in his assessment of her. His suspicions proved to be correct. For Muscarello's description of the object was virtually identical to that of the woman!

Bertrand and Muscarello then drove in the patrol car back to the field in Kensington to see if the object was still there. Several minutes later, the phone rang at the Exeter police station. Officer Toland answered it, and was nearly knocked off his chair by the voice on the other side. "My God. I see the damn thing myself!" yelled the shaking voice. It was Officer Bertrand. He and Muscarello were at the field observing the UFO as he spoke! (Fuller, 1966)

The movements of this UFO reminded me of those of the UFOs I had witnessed back at Lincoln University. Definitely signature UFO movements. There were two other UFO elements. First a geographic region involving a large body of water. The Atlantic coast was close by. Second, there was a military element. Nearby Pease Air Force base, to be exact.

Waltham, Massachusetts, 1964

This is just one of dozens of UFO reports in this area in 1964. And, like most of them, this one involved UFOs chasing military aircraft. On October 10, an unusual object was spotted over the skies of Waltham apparently pursuing two supersonic jet fighters. It was described as being a very light color, perhaps white, and was shaped like a round disk. According to witnesses on the ground, the jets appeared in the sky first, streaking across the sky and leaving a white trail behind them. The object suddenly appeared behind them, closing the distance very quickly. After catching up with the jets and pacing them for a few moments, the object emitted a bright white light, accelerated vertically, and disappeared from sight–all within about two seconds! (Fowler, 1974)

Like the Exeter sighting, this one, too, is near the Atlantic coast as well as a military facility. The facility is the Hanscom Air Force Base.

Osan Air Force Base, Korea, 1961

Osan Air Force Base in Korea was rudely awakened on the night of September 14 by an unidentified object that appeared overhead and paused there for about twelve minutes while executing various tricky maneuvers. Witnesses on the ground described it as bright, circular, with a white color that periodically changed to red. Its speed and direction were irregular. Sometimes it hovered completely motionlessly above the stunned personnel below. At other times it rose or descended vertically or lurched forward or backward horizontally. When motionless, it became very bright. When rising, its color changed to red. Finally, when a jet plane approached the area, the object darted forward, veered at a sudden ninety-degree angle, then zipped away at a tremendous speed described by the witnesses as faster than any man-made aircraft could fly. Could it be mere chance that the object chose the airspace of a military base in which to do its aerial dance? (Vallee, 1965)

Lakenheath, England, 1956

This sighting is one of the most remarkable on record because of the behavior of the UFO. On the night of August 13, the air control tower of the Skulthorpe Air Force Base was set abuzz by a strange object streaking across the landing field at tremendous speeds, estimated by radar operators at about 4,000 miles per hour. Skulthorpe reported the sighting to the Radar Air Traffic Control Center at Lakenheath some fifty miles away. Lakenheath radar operators almost immediately picked up a stationary object about twenty-five miles to the southwest, unusual at the time, because targets that were stationary or moving less than forty five knots were normally eliminated by radar screens. The operators then observed the object as it executed a dazzling string of aerial acrobatics over the next several hours. During that time, it darted around within a twenty-five mile radius at about 600 miles an hours vertically, horizontally, and in instantaneous sharp angles turns.

An RAF interceptor plane was sent up in pursuit of the object and soon made visual contact with it. Seconds later, in a breathtaking display of maneuverability, the object suddenly zipped around and behind the interceptor before the stunned pilot could even think of reacting. Realizing that he was now the hunted, the pilot tried to shake it, but couldn't. The object toyed with him, staying closely behind him and shadowing his every move. After nearly running out of fuel, the frustrated pilot headed back to the air field. The UFO, having apparently lost interest, flew northward and out of sight. (Gadd)

Did the object somehow lose its bearings and fly over the airfield by mistake? Were its aerial maneuvers over several hours a way of readjusting its instruments?

Fort Meade, Maryland, 1953-54

These were the first years of a long international wave that lasted until 1960. These two sightings were especially noteworthy, because they involve unauthorized aircraft that invaded the airspace of the highly secure Fort George G. Meade. This base housed not only the 89th AAA Battalion, but also the super secret National Security Agency. According to Army Intelligence records, on the night of December 7, 1953, Private First Class Alfred de Bonise and Sergeant First Class James Conley noticed an unusual object moving in the sky above the Battalion Headquarters. They described it as white and shiny "like a star." It was large and "shaped like a round ashtray." It also emitted an unusual sound, a kind of whirring noise. Its motion was uneven and erratic. After darting around for about twenty minutes, the object flew off in a northeasterly direction and disappeared.

The second sighting occurred on the night of April 29, 1954. The Supervisor Radio Operator along with Corporal Flath and Private First Class Hough spotted it first. They said that it flew in a straight path from the southwest and stopped directly above the Second Army Radio Station. It was round and yellowish, and emitted a blinking light. Suddenly, after being visible for about seven minutes, it stopped blinking and ascended straight up until it disappeared from view. (Good, 1988)

These sightings include a number of signature UFO elements. First, Fort Meade is a military base. Second, it is surrounded by thousands of acres of forest area. Third, nestled approximately in the middle between Baltimore, Maryland, and Washington, D.C., it is near both the Chesapeake Bay and the Potomac River. More coincidences?

The UFO Mission: Observation, Intervention and Guardianship

So, have the UFO sightings thus far suggested the reasons for alien visitations? For me the answer is an easy yes. Judging from the clearly predictable patterns of UFOs, the two immediate reasons for UFO visits are observation and intervention. Just think about it. What reason other than observation could a UFO possibly have when it hovers motionlessly and silently over a military base or a power station? Other than observation, what could a UFO possibly accomplish by pacing a man-made aircraft? In times of military conflicts, UFOs often seem to go out of their way to make themselves visible. Why? Clearly they're doing more than simply observing. The answer is a form of intervention. Dissuasion through a suggestive show of technological superiority.

Now, assuming that observation and intervention are the immediate reasons for alien visits, is there a main underlying reason for them? Are aliens observing and intervening as part of some ongoing project or plan? The answer is yes, and the project and plan can be described in one word—guardianship. Observation and intervention are functions of their overall mission as guardians of the human race! Not guardians in the sense that they have ultimate control of our destiny, however. We have developed far beyond being controlled to that extent. What I mean is guardians in a more passive sense; that is, they will continue to monitor our genetic and technological development, possibly until we reach some predesignated point in our development. Moreover, they will continue to periodically intervene in suggestive ways when we appear to be dangerous threats to one another. Will they ever intervene more actively? Perhaps, but in my opinion, only if our development begins to go drastically awry or if we reach the verge of self-annihilation through weapons of mass destruction.

For those of you who did not reach this conclusion from the evidence thus far presented and find it difficult to understand or believe, please be patient. It will become clearer and more believable during the course of this book. We will examine earlier aspects and examples of guardianship, including its beginnings, that will offer a fuller picture of this alien role and make its reality more convincingly transparent.

Close Encounters of The Fourth Kind: Abductions

These close encounters occur when there is actual physical contact with an extraterrestrial. Alien abductions are the most common form of CE-4s. Abductions are claimed to occur when extraterrestrials kidnap humans and take them aboard UFOs for various purposes, most of which involve medical examinations and, on rarer occasions, artificial insemination. What makes abductions such a controversial aspect of ufology is the fact that, despite the thousands of abduction reports, there is a significant shortage of convincing evidence. According to detractors, nearly all of what is reported is the stuff of dreams, suggestion, hoax, or hallucination. Unfortunately, there is some truth to this. We rarely if ever see the caliber of proof for abductions that we see for other types of sightings and encounters (those involving reliable witnesses, mass sightings, UFO effects, government coverups, etc...). Yet there are a handful of intriguing cases that refuse to die and demand at least a second look. One such case happens to be the first highly publicized abduction report. The one that, as they say, got the ball rolling. That of Barney and Betty Hill.

Barney and Betty Hill, 1961

It happened on the night of September 20, 1961. Driving home to Portsmouth, New Hampshire, after a vacation, Barney and Betty Hill spotted a strange glowing object gliding through the sky above them. Curious, they stopped the car, got out, and observed the object for a while, noticing that it was flying around erratically. As the object moved farther away, the Hills drove on through the White Mountains National Forest. The object was flying along the same road, U.S. Route 3, that the Hills were driving, so they continued to stop and gaze at it when it came into visual range periodically. As they approached Indian Head, the object suddenly appeared directly ahead of them and closer to the ground. So close in fact that Barney got his binoculars and was able to see the craft in vivid detail. It was shaped like a disk with small wing-like protrusions on both sides, and had a double row of windows around the front. Barney could see through the windows and observed several humanoid figures moving around inside. They were clad in black leather-like uniforms. Suddenly Barney became afraid of what might happen to him and his wife, so he jumped back into the car and drove on. Shortly thereafter, the couple remembered getting drowsy and then noticed that two hours had somehow passed by even though they had driven only 35 miles south of Indian Head.

The following day, they reported the incident to Pease Air Force Base and several days later to the National Investigations Committee on Aerial Phenomena (NICAP). A few days later, Betty began having recurring nightmares that disturbed and puzzled her. In her dreams she would see herself and Barney subjected to physical examinations by bald humanoids with tiny ears, noses and mouths and large, dark, lidless eyes. During their examination on her, the aliens took samples of her hair, ear wax, and skin scrapings, and inserted a long needle into her navel to test her for pregnancy. Finally they consulted a psychiatrist, Dr. Benjamin Simon, who hypnotically regressed them in an attempt to uncover the reason for the dreams and the missing two hours. Under hypnosis, both Hills claimed to have been abducted and subjected to the same examinations that Betty saw in her dreams. They gave almost identical descriptions of the aliens also, which were the same as Betty had described from her dreams. The most amazing aspect of their recollections under hypnosis was that their versions were nearly identical even though they were regressed separately. Evidently, as in most cases where abductions are recalled hypnotically, the abductors somehow suppressed their conscious memory of the event. (Reader's Digest)

Chariots of Gods or Demons?
The Incredible Truth About UFOs and Extraterrestrials

15

16

{Figure 15 is a drawing of the UFO seen by the Hills. Figure 16 is a photo of the Hills with a copy of a book about their experience *(The Interrupted Journey)*}

17

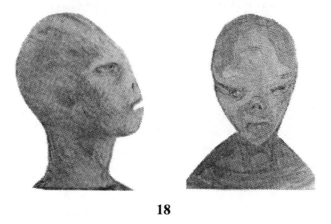

18

Figure 17 is drawing of the UFO and figure 18 of the alien abductors described by the Hills.

Detractors say that the Hill case is a product of imagination, dreams, stress, and suggestion.

Some say that the couple may have seen a UFO and then let their imagination run away with them. They also say that Barney's account under hypnosis was similar to Betty's because his *recollections* of the abduction were actually recollections of what Betty had told him about her dreams. Others say the similarities in both accounts corroborated their stories (See figures 15-18).

England, 1980

Just before dawn on November 28, Police Constable Alan Godfrey (figure 19) was cruising slowly past a housing estate in northern England, investigating reports of escaped cows roaming freely in the area. Soon he spotted a glowing object in the middle of the road ahead. Assuming it was a works bus that routinely traveled that route, he approached it, wondering why it was there so early. As he closed to within a few feet of it, however, he could see that it was no bus. Neither was it a land vehicle. It looked more like a spinning top with windows and it hovered just above the road. It had a very shiny metallic surface that reflected the image of Godfrey's car. He knew that he was witnessing something extraordinary and proceeded to sketch a picture of it. As he was doing so, however, he experienced a strange period of disorientation. One moment he was sketching the object, and the next he was driving away in the opposite direction. He didn't remember finishing the sketch or making a u-turn. He also looked at his watch and noticed that 10 minutes had inexplicably elapsed. He u-turned back in the direction of the UFO and saw that it had disappeared.

19

Godfrey left at that point, confused about what had transpired, but with a vague recollection of a strange voice telling him: "This is not for your eyes. You will forget it." Fragments of memories connected with that voice continued to plague him until, months later, he consulted a psychiatrist and underwent hypnotic regression. During the missing time, the entranced Godfrey recalled how two alien beings had taken him aboard the craft that he had seen above the road and had subjected him to a quick medical examination. Although still skeptical, the psychiatrist marveled at how consistently Godfrey's hypnotic recollections fit together. If it was a hoax, then it must have been well planned. If an hallucination, it was impressively coherent.

Fortunately, for Constable Godfrey's peace of mind and for those looking for proof of abductions, four other police officers, patrolling on foot about 8 miles from the abduction site earlier on the same morning as Godfrey's incident, had reported seeing a UFO that resembled the one described by Godfrey (see figure 20). They claimed that the object had flown so low above them that they had to duck to avoid possible contact with it. They said further that the craft then continued on in the direction of the area where Godfrey had reported seeing it. Just a series of neatly fitting coincidences? (Stuttman, vol.1)

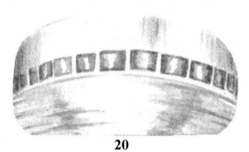

20

Argentina, 1975

Carlos Alberto Diaz had worked until about 03:30 AM on January 5, but, as of 07:00, he still had not arrived home from his job as a waiter in the town of Ingeniero White. At about that time, a passing motorist found him lying by the side of the road semi-conscious and with several patches of exposed scalp where hair had been removed. After being taken to a nearby hospital and examined, he was found to have nothing wrong with him other than the strange loss of hair. Upon being questioned by police and doctors about what had happened, Diaz related an experience that left them shaken and baffled. According to Diaz, as he was walking home, he saw a bright flash of light in front of him that he assumed was a flash of lightning. But it was brighter than lightning and blinded him temporarily. As he regained his sight moments later, he discovered that he was paralyzed. Then he felt himself being drawn upwards into the air, apparently through the bright light he had seen, towards a spherical object hovering in the sky above him. He heard a humming sound and felt a soft breezy sensation inside the beam, then fainted and awoke inside the sphere surrounded by three humanoid beings. The beings were about five-and-a-half feet tall with greenish skin, completely hairless bodies and a smooth face that appeared to have no features at all. The helpless Diaz watched in terror as the three beings extended their "stumpy" arms toward him, placed their hands on his head and somehow began extracting hair without hurting him. It was as if they were "sucking" it out. They did the same to hairy areas on his chest.

The doctors verified that the tufts of hair from his scalp and chest had been removed cleanly at the roots without causing any damage to the surrounding capillary tissues that forceful extraction would normally cause. They speculated that, somehow, whatever removed the hair had done so by creating enough suction to dilate the capillary bulbs around the roots to allow the hair shafts to come out smoothly. Interestingly enough, Diaz's watch had stopped at about 03:50 that morning. *(Flying Saucer Review*, November 1975, pp.39-42)

Parker and Hickson, 1973

21

This abduction report was a different kind in that one of the abductees claimed to be conscious during the entire experience. On October 11, 1973, as Calvin Parker and Charles Hickson were fishing near Pascagoula, Mississippi, they saw an unidentified object land nearby. They described it as bright, oval, and about 20 feet long. The two watched as three humanoids emerged who were about five feet in height and had gray wrinkled skin. Parker fainted for a short while at the sight of the beings. Both were carried by the aliens toward the ship. Suddenly they floated up and inside and found themselves in a room where they were examined by a device that resembled a huge eye. Afterwards, they both floated outside and ended up back on the riverbank. They told the local sheriff what had happened and the incident drew a lot of media attention. (Reader's Digest)

Alien Seduction? Brazil, 1957

This case is unusual, even for an abduction, because it involved the seduction of the abductee. Very early on October 15, 1957, as the 23 year old Brazilian farmer Villas Boas was tilling his soil, his tractor engine suddenly went dead. Simultaneously he noticed that a strange oval-shaped craft, about 35 feet long, was descending from the sky and landing just a few feet ahead of him. Too stunned to jump off the tractor and run, he watched in frozen fear and amazement as the three legs of the landing gear settled into the soil. Then a hatch opened and four small humanoid figures emerged dressed in one-piece uniforms and began walking toward him. Still unmoving, he watched himself being lifted by the beings and taken into the craft and into a small room with what looked like a small bed. Just as he had begun to wonder what the aliens intended to do with him, what he described as "a beautiful naked female" entered the room. At that point it was clear what to him what they wanted him to do, for they left him alone with the female. He knew that, given the circumstances, he should not have felt sexually aroused, but for some reason he couldn't help himself. His desire for the female grew with each passing second, until he could no longer restrain himself. After he separated from her, she pointed to her belly and, apparently by telepathy, made him understand that she had seduced him so that she could procreate. Shortly thereafter the other aliens returned and extracted a small amount of blood from his chin. They then escorted him out of the exit, and took off.

He told his story to friends and relatives, but was met with skepticism. Later that day, feeling strange, he went to the doctor for a checkup. Dr. Olavo Fontes reportedly found that Boas was suffering from what appeared to be mild radiation burns. He also noticed small marks on his chin where Boas had said the aliens had extracted blood. (Story).

Was this all just a fabrication by Boas? Perhaps. But if so, it was an elaborate and creative one. In addition to the stalled tractor engine, the burns and chin marks, indentations matching the UFO's pods were found in the soil where the craft had allegedly landed. Why the seduction? If it happened, perhaps it was for genetic mixing. We'll discuss that topic a little later in chapter 8.

Unfortunately these five cases are pretty much indicative of the strength of evidence presented in abduction reports. Detractors are quick to point out that it is never the prominent, high-profile citizens who claim to have been abducted, while many such people have reported *regular* (those that range from distant sightings to close encounters of the third kind) UFO sightings (Jimmy Carter, Gordon Cooper, many military officers, etc...). Of course, the British constable in the second report offers some degree of prominence. Also, there is rarely third party corroboration for abductions, such as the dozens of witnesses and radar observations that are often present with regular sightings. Fortunately, among these five accounts, three enjoy significant corroboration. Diaz and Boas displayed physical effects that appeared to support their stories. Constable Godfrey had third party corroboration, at least of the sighting. Still, unless such corroborative evidence becomes more frequent, abduction reports will continue to lack a certain degree of credibility. If it does increase, it would certainly enhance the likelihood that abductions are a real phenomenon. And if they are real, they would certainly be consistent with the guardianship mission of extraterrestrials.

Chapter 4

The Modern-Day Reappearance of UFOs

As indicated earlier, I disagree with the generally accepted notion that the modern-day reappearance of UFOs began in 1947. Compelling evidence has led me to the conclusion that it actually started during World War II. What do I mean by modern-day reappearance? Am I implying that UFOs stopped visiting us and then resumed during the second World War? Not at all. First of all, let me remind you that UFOs have been visiting us since ancient times. Second, let me strongly stress that UFOs have never *stopped* visiting us. As you recall, John Martin sighted a saucer in 1878, and there are many other documented sightings in the period between then and World War II. So why did I set the beginning of the modern era at the World War II mark? Because that is the point at which UFOs regained the widespread prominence that had previously waned.

What I mean by any UFO era is a period in which the level of UFO sightings apparently increase and gain widespread attention over an extended period of time. But not all UFO observers interpret what they see the same way. Ancient observers, of course, did not have the scientific orientation or the technological terminology to describe UFOs as flying saucers and alien spaceships. They interpreted and categorized UFOs according to the frames of reference available to them at that time. Therefore, as we will examine in subsequent chapters, UFOs were described in several very interesting ways in various UFO eras throughout our history.

World War II Sightings

For the reasons described above, World War II marked the beginning of the modern era of UFO sightings. In the early 1940s, for the first time in centuries, UFOs once again began drawing the attention of a significant portion of the human race, and interest in UFOs has grown dramatically ever since. By the way, the beginning of the modern era just happened to coincide with the most destructive war in recorded human history. Of course, we now know that such timing is not attributable to mere coincidence. The heightened and sustained level of sightings during World War II was perfectly consistent with what we know about UFO appearance patterns; namely that they appear very often in times and places of conflicts and threats. Let's now examine some of those sightings that launched the current UFO era.

James Edward Gilmer

Foo Fighters

According to several press and eyewitness accounts, corroborated by declassified government documents, from early 1942 to 1945, many World War II military pilots were chased, paced, harassed, and intimidated by strange unidentified flying objects. This is the first UFO wave of the modern era. In the section above, I mentioned that this period coincided with mankind's most destructive conflict ever. Well, that's not all it coincided with. It also marked the beginning of the greatest threat that man has ever posed to himself–the development of nuclear weapons. Recall the eerily similar time line in the events leading up to the first atomic bomb: the first self-sustaining nuclear chain reaction was initiated in December 1942 and the first atomic bomb detonated in July 1945.

No one is absolutely sure which one, but it is generally agreed that the term *foo* is either a corruption of the French word for fire, *feu*, or a play on a statement by Smokey Stover, a comic strip character, who often quipped: "Where there's foo, there's fire." Regardless of which is the actual source of the term, they both make reference to fire, and the overwhelming majority of foo fighters were described as huge globes of fire usually red or orange, or a mixture of the two. But not all unidentified flying craft that buzzed military pilots were flaming globes. Some were described as white lights and flying disks, and, rightly or wrongly, also called foo fighters. Bear in mind that, at that time, there was no official terminology to describe any UFOs, much less to differentiate one type from another. The common denominator among all foo fighters, regardless of their form, was that distraction if not intimidation was part of their apparent agenda.

In February 1942, foo fighters invaded Los Angeles airspace. Thousands of people witnessed the strange aerial shows in above them, describing them in most cases as round and emitting bright lights. These spherical objects were said to move very quickly in zig-zag motions, covering vast distances in the sky in very little time. The U.S. government was said to suspect that these objects were Japanese in origin and that Japan was preparing to use them for another attack on America.

Captain Alvah M. Reida of the 792nd Squadron, 486th Bomb Group had an unnerving encounter with a foo fighter on August 10, 1944. Shortly after completing a bombing mission in his B-29 from Ceylon to Sumatra, he and his copilot spotted an unidentified object pacing them at a distance of about 500 yards off their starboard wing. It appeared to be about circular, about 5 or 6 feet in diameter and reddish. It's shape also seemed to expand and contract in a throbbing manner. Captain Alva tried to shake the object, changing direction and altitude as quickly as possible, but to no avail. The object remained at the same position in relation to the plane regardless of what the frustrated crew did. Finally, after several minutes of frustrating the bewildered crew, the object made a sudden 90 degree turn, accelerated at an unbelievable speed, and disappeared from sight.

Chicago native Lieutenant Donald Meiers, flying in a British twin engined night fighter over the Rhine Valley in late 1944 thought the flame-colored globe pacing his Beaufighter was some new-fangled German weapon set to explode when it got close enough to them. But it didn't. It just pestered them, as it reportedly did countless other pilots. Nazi German pilots encountered them, too, and thought they were allied devices of some kind. U.S. intelligence assumed that the foo fighters seen over Germany were tools of the Nazi war machine. Pilots on bombing raids over Japan were also subjected to the antics of the foo fighters and were convinced that they were Japanese attack planes equipped with large search lights. The Japanese pilots who encountered them, believed they were secret U.S. or Russian devices used to thwart radar scans.

Gut Alt Gossen, Germany, 1944

Two prisoners of war in the custody of Nazis were working in the fields one day near Gut Alt Gossen, a town about 30 miles east of Berlin, when they had their encounter with the unknown. As they rode their tractor through nearby swamp land, the engine inexplicably stalled. They simultaneously heard a high-pitched whining noise that lasted several seconds. Although they didn't consciously perceive any cause and effect relationship between the two, they noted that the driver was able to restart the engine after the noise had stopped.

After working in the field for another 3 hours, the two spotted a strange object about 500 feet ahead of them slowly rising from the ground into the air. They described the object as a large, grayish, disk-shaped craft, about 100 yards in diameter. Shortly after coming into view, the object began emitting the same type of whine as the two men had heard earlier. Thus, it was no surprise to them when the tractor's engine stalled again. This time the cause and effect relationship was clear, so they didn't even try to restart the engine until the saucer had flown out of sight and the noise had stopped. Needless to say, the engine promptly restarted. (Fawcett)

Of course, these foo fighter and Gut Alt Gossen incidents in no way reflect the number of UFOs reported during World War II. They're just samples and illustrations of my points that 1) UFO activity increases in direct proportion to increases in conflicts and threats and 2) UFOs, in their roles as guardians, are normally either passive observers like the Gut Alt Gossen objects, or active interveners like the foo fighters.

In the next section, we will examine what, if any, effect the end of the war had on UFO activity. Do you think that the end of this conflict removed the conditions normally present during high UFO activity? If so, think again!

Post-War UFO Activity

UFO activity did not abate at the end of World War II. If anything, it increased. This is consistent with UFO behavior patterns, because, remember, World War II marked the beginning of man's greatest threat to himself and his environment–the advent of nuclear weapons. And, of course, this threat did not end in 1945, but worsened and led to the nuclear arms race. So, in retrospect, and bearing in mind the circumstances, the heightened UFO activity should surprise no one. Regarding the types and locations of UFOs sighted, these varied as much as they do during any other given period. It just so happened that one general type of UFO spotted in one general location commanded more attention than others. These attention-grabbers were dubbed *ghost rockets*, which we will examine further in the next section.

Ghost Rockets, 1946-48

The year 1946 witnessed the start of the second wave of modern UFO sightings, many of which were reported in regions from Scandinavia northward. The sightings began on or about February 26, when swarms of unidentified objects were spotted flying over northern Finland near the Arctic Circle. They were initially reported as meteors, because many of them emitted trails of various types. Some of these trails were vaporous while others were luminous.

As the sightings continued, however, the observers began realizing that not only were these not meteor swarms, but they were not natural phenomena of any type. They didn't look natural and they certainly didn't move naturally. Some were described as shining balls, cigars, eggs, missiles, and even squash rackets. The elongated shapes like cigars and missiles were by far the most frequently reported, hence the name *ghost rockets*. Regarding their movement, instead of flying steady predictable trajectories typical of meteors, they flew in ways that were anything but predictable. They flew vertically in both directions. They rolled and tumbled, zigzagged and veered at incredibly sharp angles, and usually moved at blinding speeds. When they flew in one direction long enough for an estimate, experienced pilots said they had to be flying at speeds in excess of 6,700 mph! They were clearly under intelligent control.

Later that year and on into 1948, hundreds of these mostly oblong objects were reported over several other Scandinavian countries, including Sweden and

Norway, as well as over others, like Tangier, Greece, India, and Italy. Of the countries being visited, Sweden was the most concerned. The Swedish government suspected that the ghost rockets were some type of secret weapons developed by the Soviet Union with the help of German scientists. Sweden sought to purchase America's latest radar technology to defend itself against this threat. But after carrying out some of its own investigations, the United States ruled out any connection between the objects and the Soviet Union and thus refused to sell radar technology to Sweden (see figure 85). (Jacobs, 1975; Story)

These awesome UFO spectacles seemed to represent a type of intervention. That is, rather than pacing and chasing man-made aircraft, the UFOs apparently acted in a more preemptive manner, suggestively displaying their advanced technology. If that was indeed the scope of their intentions, then mission accomplished. Like the foo fighters, the ghost rockets definitely evoked security concerns in the countries that they visited.

The Definitive Wave of the Modern Era: 1947-52

At the end of chapter 2, I mentioned that Kenneth Arnold's description of disk-shaped UFOs as *saucers* signaled the beginning of widespread public fascination with the idea of UFOs. It also marked the start of another very significant point in our recent history–the definitive wave of sightings in the modern UFO era. Definitive in the sense that it was more responsible than any other wave before or since in bringing mankind's collective awareness and objective knowledge of UFOs to the point where it is today. Subsequent waves have added relatively little new information and have largely served to confirm what we learned in that wave. In prior waves, UFOs were certainly noticed, but, generally speaking, neither objectively recognized nor properly categorized as what they really were, namely flying vehicles composed of physical materials and controlled by intelligent mortal beings of extraterrestrial origin. Remember, during World War II, foo fighters, ghost rockets and UFOs of other shapes were generally considered secret weapons built by hostile nations. In much earlier eras, people had other more supernatural views of UFOs, which we will examine a little later. For now, let's take a look at some of the sightings that made this wave so significant.

Before we start, please bear in mind that we'll examine a mere handful from among thousands of documented sightings reported from all over the world during this wave. Regarding its unusually extended length, some Ufologists believe this six-year wave is composed of not one long wave but several smaller waves and flaps. From my perspective, both are valid views. On the one hand, considering the sustained frequency of sightings during this time, I chose to follow the lead of Jacques Vallee and other researchers who prefer to group them together into one long wave. On the other hand, as you will see in the following reports, there are distinct enough differences in the types and locations of sightings to warrant their separation into smaller periods. For these reasons, I prefer to think of the entire 6-year period as a *superset* wave and the smaller ones as its *subsets*. The following are just a sampling of that period.

The Roswell Crash, New Mexico, July, 1947

This was one of the highest-activity years ever documented for UFO sightings and should be considered a separate wave. The most famous UFO incident of 1947 also happens to be the most famous and controversial one thus far in the modern era: the UFO crash near Roswell, New Mexico. It's an unusual case, too, because it involves a UFO crash Some call it the most convincing evidence ever seen that UFOs are real. Others, particularly the U.S. government, still maintain that, while something did crash, it wasn't a UFO. You be the judge.

(Roswell Daily Record's lead article on the Roswell crash)

To put the Roswell crash in its proper perspective, let's briefly review what happened in the days immediately preceding it. Within two weeks of the Kenneth Arnold sighting on June 24, 1947, the term flying saucer had caught on and become a permanent fixture in the English language, as thousands of such objects were reportedly seen in several states during that period. What's more, unidentified objects flying in very fast and unusual patterns were being simultaneously tracked on radar screens, especially near Roswell, New Mexico. The sightings and radar trackings in that area had become so frequent that the federal government had sent officials to investigate. The following summary of

Chariots of Gods or Demons?
The Incredible Truth About UFOs and Extraterrestrials

the Roswell incident is a distillation of the accounts of several sources, including Timothy Good, H.S. Stuttman, Reader's Digest, and others.

Shortly before ten o'clock on the night of July 2, 1947, two very respected citizens of Roswell, Mr. And Mrs. Dan Wilmot were sitting on their porch chatting and enjoying the clear starry sky. Suddenly Mr. Wilmot spotted a large glowing object streaking across the sky at a high rate of speed in a northwesterly direction. He quickly called his wife's attention to it, and they both ran down into the yard to get a better look. They described it as rather oval in shape, like two inverted saucers placed together mouth to mouth. It was at least 20 feet in diameter, although it was hard to tell given the darkness and the fact that the object was approximately 1,500 feet up. It was brightly luminous, as though illuminated from the inside, and made no noise, except for a "swishing" sound for a short while. The entire sighting lasted about a minute.

Later that night, in the same general area, an unidentified object being tracked by local radar suddenly dropped off the screen and was presumed to have crashed. A local rancher named William Brazel stated that he had heard a very loud explosion near his property that night, but believed that it was likely a loud thunderclap.

23

The next morning, Brazel went to the area where he thought he had heard the noise and discovered extensive wreckage from some type of crashed object spread out over nearly a mile on his ranch. He first contacted local Sheriff George Wilcox, who advised him to notify the military. Military units quickly arrived and sealed off the entire area. While crash debris was being loaded into transport vehicles, Major Jesse Marcel (see figure 23), intelligence officer at the 509th Bomb Group at Roswell Army Air Field (RAAF) was sent to investigate. Marcel and Brazel described the wreckage as some type of metal unlike anything they had ever seen before. It was thin, lightweight, and flexible, but could not be burned by extreme heat. And when hit with hammer blows, the dents would gradually smooth out. Some of the pieces were also inscribed with characters that Marcel described as hieroglyphics.

Not yet ordered to proceed in any secretive manner with the press, RAAF Commander Colonel William Blanchard instructed his press officer, William Haut, to release a statement announcing that the 509th Bomb Group had

recovered the wreckage of a flying disk of presumably extraterrestrial origin (See figure 24). Shortly after the press article was released, federal investigators reportedly began ordering all Roswell witnesses to remain silent about it, using direct and indirect threats. Many researchers regard this as the beginning of a coverup that has yet to be lifted.

Marcel was stupefied by what happened next. After being assigned to oversee the air transport of the wreckage to Wright Field (now Wright-Patterson Air Force Base) in Ohio, his transport plane made an interim stop at Carswell Air Base in Fort Worth, Texas. Once there, he was relieved of his assignment by the Commander of the 8th Army Air Force, Brigadier General Roger Ramey, warned with indirect threats to keep quiet about the crash, and ordered back to Roswell. After sending the UFO debris on to Wright Field, Ramey hastily called a press conference at which he recanted the earlier article about the flying disk and presented pieces of a weather balloon, stating that these were what had actually been found near Roswell.

24
(Ramey with weather balloon debris)

25

(Press article on Ramey's recant of government statement that saucer had crashed)

Could Colonel Blanchard and all of his experts at RAAF have mistaken a weather balloon for something as clearly different as a flying disk? Since the crash, dozens of other highly credible eyewitnesses, military and civilian, have come forward as witnesses to a UFO crash at Roswell, and their accounts are nearly identical. Did they all conspire to weave such a tall tale? Were the numerous visual and radar sightings in that same area all hoaxes, hallucinations or coincidences? Incidentally, after years of being unable to explain how alien bodies came to be found among the wreckage of a so-called weather balloon, the Pentagon, finally came forward publicly in the late 1990's with the official statement that the bodies found were those of life-sized manikins that had been dropped for crash test purposes!

Assuming that it was a UFO that crashed at Roswell, did it just happen to be there at that time? Was it mere coincidence that a UFO flap was already underway in that area? Before you reply, consider the following facts about the Roswell area: First of all, it was home to a military base, the Roswell Army Air Field. The RAAF, in turn, housed the 509th Bomber Group, the only bomber group entrusted at that time with the storage and delivery of atomic bombs. The *Enola Gay,* the bomber that delivered the atomic bomb that devastated Hiroshima, was part of the 509th. Also recall that the test site for atomic bombs and rockets was just a hundred miles from Roswell, at the Alamogordo Army Air Field (now Holloman Air Force Base) and the White Sands Proving Ground (now White Sands Missile Range). The first atomic bomb was detonated on July 16, 1945 at a spot in the northwest corner of these testing areas now known as Trinity Site. Both testing areas are nestled between the Sacramento Mountains to the east and the San Andreas and Organ Mountains to the west. Just northeast of Roswell is Cannon Air Force Base, and a little farther in that direction is Los Alamos National Laboratory where the first atomic and hydrogen bombs were developed.

These facts should ring at least two bells in your mind regarding UFO sighting patterns. One, there are three nearby mountain ranges, which are one of the geographic areas frequented by UFOs. Two, bearing in mind our earlier discussion about the tendency of UFOs to frequent areas of conflict and threat, you have probably figured out by now that military bases in general are UFO magnets. Furthermore, this *magnetism* seems to increase in proportion to the scope of the potential threats. And how much more threatening could an area be than the Roswell area, which contains not only several military bases, but also facilities for the development, testing, storage, and delivery of atomic bombs and missiles!

The Mantell Case, Kentucky, 1948

Many people believe this incident provided even stronger evidence of extraterrestrial visitors than did the Roswell crash. It involved the first confirmed death of a person directly related to a UFO. It also provided the first real-time description of a UFO while it was being observed. Again, you decide.

At about 1:25 pm on January 7, 1948, just six months after the Roswell crash, tower officials at Godman Air Field in Kentucky spotted a large unidentified disk-shaped object hovering overhead. They alerted the base Commander, Colonel Guy Hicks, who joined them as they sat in amazement watching the object for nearly ninety minutes through binoculars. It was broad daylight, and the object was also visible to many other people in the general area, including the Kentucky State Police. At about 2:35 pm, a trio of F-51 Mustangs led by Captain Thomas Mantell, flying overhead at the time en route to another location, was asked to intercept and investigate the object. Mantell complied, and led the planes in pursuit of the object, which by now had begun to move away. After closing in enough to observe it in detail he described it, among other things, as "metallic...tremendous in size, ...and very bright."

After they reached about 15,000 feet one of the planes developed trouble with its oxygen equipment and broke off the chase. At about 22,000 feet, Mantell's other companion plane dropped out due to oxygen problems. So Mantell proceeded alone, chasing the UFO for another half hour, all the while continuing his radio descriptions of the object. His trouble apparently began after he had risen above 30,000 feet trying to "get a better look at it." It is generally believed that he suffered oxygen deprivation at that point. At any rate, his plane suddenly spiraled downward and crashed. It is still being debated whether his plane exploded while still in the air or upon impact with the ground. That UFO was seen by many witnesses for several days after the Mantell crash.

Chariots of Gods or Demons?
The Incredible Truth About UFOs and Extraterrestrials

26

(Drawing of Mantell's chase after the UFO)

Immediately after word of Mantell's death went public, controversy raged over what he had really seen. According to the first official explanation, it was actually the planet Venus, which can appear bright in the sky under the right atmospheric conditions. This was soon proven false, however, because an investigation showed that the position of the planet Venus was much too low in the sky to appear above Mantell and the other two planes. Furthermore, Venus would have never appeared as large as the object seen by Mantell's flight and many observers on the ground. The government then tried the weather balloon explanation again, stating that a balloon had been released at about the time of the sighting to test very high atmospheric conditions. While it is true that weather balloons were in use in that general time frame, there were no records of one being deployed at the time or in the area of the Mantell incident.

So was this a mass hallucination shared by civilians, state police, Mantell, and the other military personnel? Did the Godman Air Field Tower crew and Colonel Hicks all suffer the same illusion, even though they observed the object with binoculars for over an hour? I don't think so, and my guess is that you probably don't either. Assuming that the UFO was real, I think it's safe to assume that it was hovering over Godman Air Field for observational purposes.

Southeast Asia, 1948

UFO activity in Southeast Asia seemed to reach a peak in 1948. One example occurred on August 1. After numerous reported sightings throughout Southeast Asia that day, the crew of a plane that included a French radio-television news correspondent named Samy Simon spotted a large metallic, "fish-shaped" object moving near them as they flew over Saigon. They estimated its size at about twice that of a large bomber. They also reported seeing another unidentified object of similar size and shape flying just beneath it, which appeared to match the movements of the first. Already flying at a rather fast pace, the objects suddenly made sharp turns of about 90 degrees without slowing down. They then disappeared from view. (Vallee, 1965)

It's more than mere chance that the 1947-52 wave coincided so neatly with the French-Indochina War of 1946-54. One fact that makes this crystal clear to me is the unusually high number of UFO sightings reported there during that period. And it goes without saying that the UFO activity was directly related to the conflict and threat posed by the war.

New Mexico, 1948-50

Like 1947, this period teemed with documented UFO sightings, and, like 1947, it could be called a separate wave period. By now, the U.S. government had begun considering these strange intruders a very real and potentially dangerous phenomenon. The most alarming thing about their incursions was the fact that they were obviously targeting the government's high-security facilities around the state. By 1950, the situation had escalated to the point where the Air Force had launched a joint investigation of UFO activity in the area with a firm called Land-Air, Inc.of Alamogordo, New Mexico. After numerous sightings, radar trackings, photographs, and written reports, the investigation concluded that "...the unexplained...fireballs and disks are still observed in the vicinity of sensitive military and Government installations..." A similar Air Force investigation and report entitled "Summary of Aerial Phenomena in New Mexico," also written in 1950, added further descriptions of the objects as "...green fireballs, objects moving at high speeds in shapes resembling half moons, circles and disks emitting...light." These lights varied greatly in color.

One of these UFO visits occurred on April 24, 1949 over the White Sands Proving Ground. That afternoon, a government official there, Charles Moore, was checking the flight patterns of weather balloons that had just been released. While peering through his theodolite at one particular balloon, he spotted a strange object flying slowly near the balloon, almost hovering beside it. It was elliptical and convex in shape, like two oblong ash trays pressed together at their rims. It was rather large, and made no noticeable sounds. After a few seconds of apparently observing the balloon, the object glided away and disappeared into the clouds. Moore's sighting was confirmed by five other witnesses present at that time. (Fawcett)

The main significance of all these sightings in New Mexico, again, involves the areas in which they occur, which are consistent with UFO patterns. As described above and in the section on Roswell, these UFO visits are clearly connected to the military and government installations sprinkled around this state and to the potential threat that they represent.

Oak Ridge, Tennessee, 1950

This was an extremely busy year for UFOs in many places around the world, including the Oak Ridge area. It was also another very troubling one for the U.S. government, because, as in New Mexico, these unidentified flying objects were intruding on an extremely sensitive facility. This time it was the area's testing facility for the Atomic Energy Commission, which is mainly operational from late spring through winter. During this period, dozens of UFO sightings in the area were documented, most of which were corroborated by numerous eyewitnesses. The reports ranged from those of ordinary civilians walking the streets to radar-confirmed reports of high-ranking military personnel stationed in the area. One of these reports was submitted on October 24 by William B. Fry, Assistant Chief of Security for the Nuclear Energy for Propulsion of Aircraft project (NEPA) at the Oak Ridge facility. While at an Oak Ridge drive-in theater with his wife and child at about 6:45 that evening, he spotted a glowing object at about 40 degrees above the North-Northwest horizon. The object was circular and emitted a light that changed to various colors, including, green, blue, red, and orange. It swung back and forth in a soft pendulum motion, but hung basically over the same area. It continued this dazzling display for the next half hour and then glided silently away into the darkness. (Fawcett)

Fry's sighting was corroborated by his family and the drive-in projectionist, as well as by simultaneous showings on the radar screen at the Knoxville Airport Radar Site.

An Astronaut's Sightings, Europe, 1951

It is completely understandable that the people who see UFOs most often and most clearly are people who travel through the air like UFOs. These people, of course, are pilots and astronauts. Although most members of these groups are very reluctant to publicly announce their sightings for fear of ridicule and losing their jobs, there are some brave individuals, who place our right to know the truth above such risks. One such astronaut and U.S. Air Force pilot is none other than Gordon Cooper (see figure 27)! In statements presented to the United Nations in 1978, Cooper revealed that, while he was a fighter pilot, stationed in Germany in 1951, he and several other pilots witnessed UFOs on several occasions over Germany and other European areas: "Several days in a row we sighted groups of metallic, saucer-shaped vehicles at great altitudes over the base and we tried to get close to them, but they were able to change direction faster than our fighters..." (Good)

27

The UFO activity reported by Cooper over Germany was consistent with the UFO tendency to frequent areas of conflict and threat. Recall the hotbed of sporadic conflicts and perpetual threats spawned by the cold war in Europe.

The Lubbock Lights, Texas, 1951

From late summer to early fall 1951, witnesses in the general vicinity of Lubbock reported numerous sightings of what appeared to be a large, wing-shaped object flying overhead. It was described as having blueish lights that traced the contours of its horizontal V shape (see figure 28).

There are indications that these UFO incursions may be connected with earlier sightings in the area of Albuquerque, New Mexico. Such a connection would be no surprise, of course, since, as you recall, New Mexico had been a hotbed of UFO sightings since the start of the modern era, especially near military and other government installations, such as White Sands Proving Ground and the Atomic Energy Commission installation in Albuquerque. The first sighting of what was later called the Lubbock lights occurred on August 25 over Albuquerque and was reported by none other than an official of the Atomic Energy Commission! This official and his wife estimated the object's altitude at about 1000 feet and described it as wing-shaped with blueish lights along its rear and blueish-green lights along its "wings."

What must have been just minutes later that same evening, a group of college professors in Lubbock, Texas, spotted what may have been the same "object," as their description was virtually identical to that of the official in Albuquerque. Over the next few hours, the UFO left and returned several times, reported by various people in different areas of town. During these sightings, witnesses began calling into question the assumption that the UFO was a single wing-shaped craft. According to some, instead of remaining like a V, it began assuming other shapes, which seemed to create a conflict in the descriptions reported. The conflict was eventually resolved however: After the strange lights were sighted and photographed for several more days, it was ascertained that they were not attached to one large object, but were actually emitted by separate smaller craft. The Lubbock lights turned out to be individual disk-shaped craft flying in a V formation (see figure 28)! This is reminiscent of many other sightings, including mine, where set UFO formations are spotted.

(Photo of the Lubbock lights)

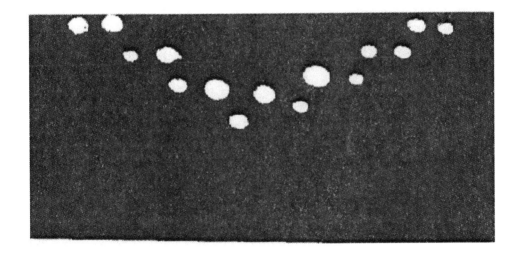

28

The Wave of 1952

This year was as at least as eventful as 1947, many say even more so, in terms of the number of sightings reported worldwide. In either case, 1952 qualifies as another separate wave. On January 30, a gigantic disk that spun like a huge horizontal wheel was observed for several minutes in the skies over Korea. On May 20, a large disk-shaped object appeared over Denham, England

and released several smaller objects of identical shape which quickly scattered in various directions.

The 1952 Flap Over Washington, D.C.

During the final two weeks of July, large groups of disk-shaped objects made two spectacular visits to Washington, D.C., flying over the Capitol and the White House. Timothy Good correctly refers to this period as the *July 1952 flap.* Although UFOs also buzzed other U.S. locations during that time, the two over D.C. were clearly the most visible. The first, as Good recounts, occurred on 19 July. That night, UFOs came in breathtaking numbers, hovering, cruising, flying at a snail's pace, then suddenly accelerating to lightning speeds. Numerous spectators on the ground and pilots in the air reported the intruders and several radar stations tracked them.

(A scene from the 1950s movie *Earth vs The Flying Saucers*, based on leaked word of a government coverup of UFOs)

After a lengthy visit that night, the UFOs left Washington D.C. and returned on 26 July. This time they were even more impressive with their uncanny speed and maneuverability. Again they were spotted by witnesses and tracked on radar. A few jets were deployed to investigate the sightings, but had no chance of actually catching up with them. The U.S. Air Force released a detailed report on these sightings in 1985.

Chariots of Gods or Demons?
The Incredible Truth About UFOs and Extraterrestrials

30

(Air traffic controllers watching their radarscope at National Airport during the 1952 July flap in Washington, D.C.)

NATO Exercises, English Channel, 1952

As impressive as the Washington, D.C., sightings were, the most well-documented and significant sightings of 1952 are likely the ones that occurred over the Atlantic Ocean in September. Shortly after 7:00 p.m. On September 20TH, during a series of NATO exercises called "Operation Mainbrace", a strange unidentified object was seen following close behind the NATO fleet. Three photographs taken by observers revealed a large disk-shaped object with a grayish metallic hue. After several minutes of pacing the fleet, it flew by and disappeared. Later that day, an object of identical description was reported flying slowly over Denmark's largest military air base. On September 24, following an incredible flurry of sightings all over Europe, Operation Mainbrace was paid another personal visit by a UFO. Like the first time, it caught up with the fleet and paced it from behind. This time, instead of a flying disk, it was a spherical object. After several encounters with UFOs, the fleet was ready this time with a jet fighter which gave immediate chase. The jet's crew drew near enough to the object to get a clear look at it, describing it as a "whitish-silvery sphere that revolved around its axis." After a few seconds, the object zipped away at a high rate of speed before the crew could make further observations.

There are clearly two general connections to be made here regarding UFO patterns. The most obvious is the fact that the NATO forces were engaged in war-like activities, which frequently attract UFOs. Second, as we mentioned earlier, large bodies of water are the geographic areas most visited by UFOs. And the Atlantic Ocean is quite large.

Chapter 5

Pre-Modern And Ancient Sightings

As mentioned earlier, reports of UFO sightings did not just recently begin, but actually date back even farther than mankind's oldest written records, if one acknowledges the prehistoric drawings of what appear to be UFOs and aliens on the walls of caves around the world. Many of these ancient images have unmistakable similarities. One cave painting resembling an astronaut was discovered in Australia over 3000 years ago (figure 31). Another, estimated to be about 8000 years old, was painted on the walls of an African cave in Tassili in the Sahara Desert (figure 33). Still another was found in a cave in Italy (figure 32). All of these drawings depict humanoid figures wearing one-piece suits, domed transparent helmets that completely enclose the head, and possibly protruding antenna. Compare these images to that of the modern astronaut in figure 34. Startling similarities?

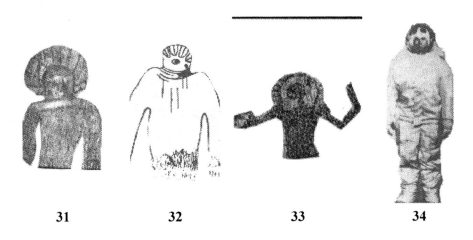

31   32   33   34

A very significant fact that emerges from written reports of pre-modern and ancient UFO sightings is that their patterns are generally consistent with the recent ones that we've ascertained. That is, for the most part, they exhibited the guardianship patterns of observation and interference, especially in areas of conflict and threat. And, as in modern sightings, they tended to be seen disproportionately near mountains, forests, and large bodies of water and ice. Let's review a few of them, again bearing in mind that these are just a brief sampling of the thousands of reported sightings.

James Edward Gilmer

The UFO Wave of 1896-97

During this period, American and Canadian newspapers were filled with articles on reported sightings of these strange craft that traveled through the air. Although their specific appearances varied, their general shape seemed to be fairly consistent: Most were oblong, like cigars and barrels. Another consistent feature was that lights of various colors were emitted from the underside of the the craft at night. The first of such sightings were reported in November 1896 in western North America, mainly in California, Washington (state) and Canada. In one California sighting, a UFO was seen descending, rising, and then flying out of sight (see figure 35).

35

(San Francisco newspaper story and illustration of a 22 November 1896 UFO sighting)

Curiously enough, as sightings began to be reported in areas to the east, the ones in certain areas of the west either slackened dramatically or ceased altogether. For example, the beginning of 1897 marked not only the start of sightings in Nebraska, but also the end of those in California. Soon thereafter, UFOs were reported in several others states, including Kansas, Missouri and Michigan. According to various newspaper accounts, 10,000 Missouri residents witnessed a huge black object hovering in the sky above them. The *Chicago Record* wrote that the "object appeared very swiftly, then appeared to stop and hover over Kansas City for ten minutes at a time, then after flashing green-blue and white lights, shot upwards into space." Kansas (state) residents described one of their UFOs as measuring an estimated 25 to 30 feet long and having the shape of a canoe with "a searchlight of varying colors." Eventually, such UFO sightings were reported over most of the states until about May of 1897. (Story)

Turkey, 1885

Witnesses in Adrianople, Turkey, reported on November 1, 1885 that a strange object had drifted slowly across the sky at about 9:30 that night. Flying just west of Adrianople, the object's size was estimated at about five times that of the moon's orb, and its shape was oblong. It apparently made no noise and emitted a glow so bright that it illuminated a large area on the surface areas that it passed over. (Vallee, 1965)

Northwest Africa, 1870

Initially, Captain F.W. Banner of the British ship *Lady of the Lake* thought he was viewing an unusual cloud formation. It was late afternoon on March 22, 1870, off the coast of northwest Africa, and his crew had called his attention to the peculiar object hovering among the clouds above them. Almost immediately after spotting it they had begun to doubt that it was just another cloud. Banner compared it to a circular cloud "with an included semi-circle divided into four parts and a central shaft running from the center of the circle and extending far outward and curving backward..." After several more minutes of amazement, their doubts became full reality. They were convinced that it wasn't a cloud. A decisive factor in this conclusion was that the object was "traveling against the wind." Banner noted that it moved from the south and "settled right into the wind's eye." The object hovered visibly above the confused crew until the evening grew too dark and it could no longer be seen. (Wilkins, p.217)

London, 1742

On the evening of December 16, 1742, a fellow of the Royal Society had just left a meeting and was enroute to his home when he spotted something in the dark sky above that froze him in his tracks. He made the following observations about what he saw:

"...a light arose from behind the trees and houses, to the south and west, which at first I thought was a rocket, of large size. But when it rose 20 degrees, it moved parallel to the horizon, and ((moved in a gentle fluttering pattern)) and went on in the direction of north by east. It seemed very near. Its motions was very slow. I had it for about half a mile in view. A light flame was turned backward by the resistance the air made to it. From one end, it emitted a bright glare and fire that that of burning charcoal. That end was a frame like bars of iron, and quite opaque to my sight. At one point, on the longitudinal frame, or cylinder, issued a train in the shape of a tail of light more bright at one point on the rod or cylinder, and growing gradually fainter at the end of the rod of cylinder; so that it was transparent for more than half of its length. The head of this strange object seemed about half a degree in diameter ((about the size of the moon's orb)), and the tail near three degrees in length." (Reader's Digest)

So what the observer saw was an oblong-shaped UFO that emitted a fiery trail and flew in an erratic fluttering manner. He signed his report with the initials C.M., indicating that even in the 18th century, UFO witnesses preferred to remain anonymous rather than to risk ridicule.

Nuremberg, 1561; Basel, 1566

The sighting in Nuremberg, Germany, near the Pegnitz River, was one of the more notable in the history of documented UFO activity, because of the sheer number of witnesses. On April 14, dozens of strange aerial craft mesmerized and terrorized virtually the entire city of Nuremberg with a frightening display of ungodly capabilities. The daunting objects came in several shapes and sizes, including long tubes, spheres, cigars, and disks, as well as fiery crosses. The bewildered onlookers on the ground feared for their lives and sought divine safety in churches and cathedrals. Huddling together and expecting destruction at any moment, some of the braver people peered through windows and watched in horror as the things in the skies continued to maneuver very closely and erratically in relation to one another as though they were engaged in some type of exercise or possibly a battle among themselves. This incident was recorded not only in written documents, but in paintings and drawings as well. These artistic works are presently located in the Nuremberg Library.

The objects sighted in Basel, Switzerland on August 7,1566 reportedly exhibited the same behavior, but involved objects that were almost exclusively large circular objects.

Japan, 1235 A.D.

On September 24, a Japanese officer ordered what might be the first official UFO investigation in recorded history. While General Yoritsume and his army were encamped that night, they spotted strange lights in the sky dancing about in dazzling displays of maneuverability. They looped, circled, swung, and zipped around for several hours in the southwestern sky. Yoritsume ordered a "full-scale investigation" of the objects on the spot. Apparently unwilling to offer an explanation outside their familiar realms of thinking, Yoritsume's officials handed him one that read: "the whole thing is completely natural, General. It is…only the wind making the stars sway." (Vallee, 1969) Note the fact that the UFO pilots chose to carry out their maneuvers directly above a military encampment.

Gempeii War, Japan, 1180

During this Japanese civil war, which pitted the Taira and Minamoto clans against each other, a close Japanese equivalent to the term flying saucer was used to describe an unidentified flying object seen in the dark skies above. On the night of October 27, observers reported the sighting of a luminous object that resembled a flying "earthenware vessel." It was first spotted in the northeast coming from a mountain in the Kii province. (Vallee, 1969)

This sighting contains both general types of patterns. That is, the object was spotted during a conflict and it was seen coming from a typical geographic area. This time a mountain.

Jerusalem, 11th Century

At the end of the 11th century, during the first Crusade, strange bright objects were seen flying over the night skies of Jerusalem. Not knowing what to make of them, the frightened observers below considered them part of some hostile military force. From a modern-day perspective, these objects would have been viewed as UFOs flying in formation. To 11th century witnesses, however, these multicolored objects were infernal armies "marching in the sky." (Vallee, 1965)

By their repeated appearances in the same area, the objects were obviously intent on making themselves visible during the siege of Jerusalem, which, of course, is reminiscent of other forms of interference that we have reviewed.

France, 8th-10th Centuries

During the reigns of Pepin the Short and Charlemagne during the 8th and 9th centuries A.D., respectively, unidentifed flying objects began an extensive string of incursions into what is now France. Predictably, the objects were particularly visible during the military campaigns of both rulers. After the extensive military conquests of Charlemagne, UFO reports subsided somewhat. UFO activity peaked again during the Magyar raids in France in the 10th century, appearing very frequently over Verdun and Reims. From the beginning, these bright objects in the sky were referred to as *fiery armies* and were considered by French rulers as emissaries sent by their enemies. They also believed that, in order to fly, the ships had to be involved with supernatural forces. These "tyrants of the air" were so feared, and their visitations became so frequent, that the French sovereignty began to issue and enforce severe *penalties against creatures that travel on aerial ships* and even people who reported sightings of them!

Charlemagne, 810 A.D.

As indicated in the previous section, UFOs were frequent visitors to the realm of Charlemagne. One of those times was in 810. It happened six years after the 68 year old monarch had retired from active battle, but when his forces were still warring against Danes and other Saxons who had refused to stop their resistance following their defeat at the hands of Charlemagne in 804. According to historian St. Gregory of Tours in his *Historia Francorum*, Charlemagne's personal secretary and biographer Alcuin, author of *Vita Karoli*, had reported that one day, as Charlemagne had just left his capital city of Aachen (Aix-la-Chapelle in French), he sighted a huge circular object flying above him. It flew westward and shone so brightly that his horse reared up, causing him to fall and injure himself severely.

England, 776 A.D.

It happened during the reign of Offa, who had become ruler over Anglo-Saxon England after avenging the murder of his cousin, King Aethelbald. The wars were frequent and fought for various reasons. Some to subdue resistors, others to quash revolts, and still others to discipline law breakers. According to a translation of the *Annales Laurissenses* for the year 776, rebellious Saxons were in the process of storming a castle fortress when they suddenly froze, transfixed at what they beheld in the sky above them. Witnesses reported "two large shields" flying above the fortress. They were reddish and seemed to be hovering directly over the fortress church. The pagan Saxons then fled, having interpreted the appearance of the objects as a sign of divine intervention on behalf of the Christians inside the fortress.

It's fairly clear that the imagery used here describing the objects as *shields* comes about as close as one could get to the more modern *disks* and *saucers* using 8th century terminology.

Roman Empire, 1st-3rd Centuries B.C.

Roman author Julius Obsequens included several reports of UFO sightings in his book *Prodigorium Liber*. The following are a few examples:

In 216 B.C., during the Second Punic War (also called the Hannibalic War), a host of UFOs were seen flying in the skies above the battles. They were described as "things like ships...seen in the sky over Italy...east of Rome, a *round shield* was seen in the sky." This was a peak year of UFO sightings, and, interestingly enough, also one that witnessed the bloodiest battle of the entire war (Hannibal's forces slaughtered about 60,000 Roman soldiers). Just a coincidence?

During the Second Servile War (Slave War in Sicily), reports of UFO sightings reached a high point in 99 B.C. According to Obsequens, "there fell in different places...a thing like a flaming torch, and it came suddenly from the sky. Towards sunset, a round object like a *globe*, or round or circular *shield* took its path in the sky, from west to east."

In 90 B.C., during the second Social War (also called War of the Allies or Marsic War), globes of fire (recall *foo fighters*) were seen flying overhead. On one occasion, as Obsequens recounts, a golden-colored globe "fell to the earth, gyrating. It then seemed to increase in size, rose from the earth, and ascended into the sky, where it obscured the disk of the sun with its brilliance. It revolved towards the eastern quadrant of the sky." (Wilkins, 1954)

Alexander the Great, 336 B.C.-323 B.C.

To say that Alexander's reign was a militarily active one borders on an understatement. Predictably, and consistent with UFO patterns, reports of sightings increased greatly during his conquests. On several occasions, Alexander himself reported seeing *flying shields* that hovered above his battle sites and followed his troops for great distances between battles. But he wasn't a typical UFO witness of that era. His views of UFOs seemed to be somewhat more objective than those commonly held then. Some ufologists believe it was because he had made actual contact with aliens. He was rumored to have flown in a UFO at least once. In his description of that flight, he told how the earth below him looked as he rose above it. Among other things, he said that some large bodies of water assumed a serpentine appearance as he gained in altitude. Some researchers believe such descriptions validate the notion that Alexander indeed flew, because he couldn't have been so accurate in his descriptions without actually done so. Finally, Alexander apparently believed that there were other inhabited planets besides earth. In response to the notion that he had conquered all the known world, Alexander reportedly opined to his warriors that there were worlds beyond this one that he would never conquer. (Reader's Digest)

Pharaoh Thutmose III, Egypt, 1469 B.C.

This is one of the earliest written reports of a UFO sighting. Excerpted from an Egyptian papyrus, (see figure 37) it formed part of the annals of Thutmose III (figure 36), who reigned circa 1504-1450 B.C. Although just one of the many sightings reported in that era, this one was particularly noteworthy because of its timing and the attention that it received from the Pharaoh himself. It occurred during the first Battle of Megiddo in about 1469. Seeking to regain Egypt's former military prominence, Thutmose led his armies in a successful sweep through the Middle East in the 1470s, restoring Egyptian control of Palestine. But

James Edward Gilmer

36

in 1469, when marching toward the northern Palestinian city of Megiddo, the gateway to Mesopotamia, he encountered unexpectedly stiff opposition from enemy forces there. Undeterred, he laid a successful seven-month siege to the city, and it was then that these particular UFOs were spotted. The following excerpt was taken from a translation by Prince Boris de Rachewiltz:

"In the...third month of winter, sixth hour of the day...the scribes of the House of Life found it was a circle of fire that was coming in the sky...His Majesty was meditating upon what had happened. Now after some days had passed, these things became more numerous in the sky than ever. They shone more in the sky than the brightness of the sun and extended to the limits of the four supports of the heavens...Powerful was the position of the fire circles. The army of the Pharaoh looked on with him in their midst...It was after supper...And what happened was ordered by the Pharaoh to be written in the annals of the House of Life...so that it be remembered forever." (Le Poer Trench, 1966)

Chariots of Gods or Demons?
The Incredible Truth About UFOs and Extraterrestrials

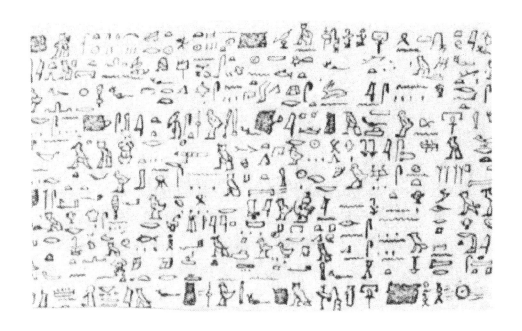

37
(Over 3,400 years old, this Egyptian papyrus reports the sighting of numerous strange luminous flying objects witnessed by Pharaoh Thutmose III, his army, and others in his empire.)

38

Biblical UFO Sightings?

Did Ezekiel See a UFO?

What was it that Ezekial saw that day? A divine vision as he reported in the first chapters of the Old Testament book of Ezekiel (as seen in the 18th century depiction in figure 38)? Biblical scholars who would normally interpret such visions as symbolic are at a loss to explain or even hazard a good guess as to what symbolism is being used in this instance. Many ufologists feel that no explanation of the symbolism can be given because none is involved. Ezekiel described exactly what he thought he saw, but what he actually saw near the Chebar river in Chaldea in about 593 B.C. was a UFO, they say. They believe that his other three visions also involved UFOs, but we'll limit this discussion to the first one, since it is the one most elaborately described.

Ufologists call attention to the fact that Ezekiel perceived the object through the filter of his religious mindset and described it using the limited terminology of his era, making the object seem more unreal than if someone living today had described it. What's more, some even believe that if what Ezekiel saw were built using his descriptions, with a few terminology tweaks, the result would be a fully functional vehicle. Does that sound far-fetched? Well, it just so happens that a NASA engineer by the name of Josef F. Blumrich did just that. He constructed and patented a fully functional machine using part of Ezekiel's description as a guide. He said what landed in Ezekiel's presence was similar to what we would call a landing craft today. Let's review what Ezekiel said about the object, and then see what Blumrich had to say about it.

First of all, note that the end of chapter 1, verse 1 reads: "...the heavens were opened, and I saw visions of God."

Some ufologists point out that these words are indicative of a virtually invariable practice among ancient people to view inexplicable aerial phenomena as divine in origin (We will review this practice in more detail in the section on mythology in chapter 7 of this book). Therefore, whether a vision or a UFO sighting, Ezekiel, like any other person living during his time would have connected it to God, because it came from the sky. Starting at the fourth verse, Ezekiel described his vision as follows:

4) And I looked, and, behold, a whirlwind came out of the north, a great cloud, and a fire infolding itself, and a brightness was about it, and out of the midst thereof as the colour of amber; out of the midst of the fire.
5) Also out of the midst thereof came the likeness of four living creatures. And this was their appearance; they had the likeness of a man.
6) And every one had four faces, and every one had four wings.
7) And their feet were straight feet; and the sole of their feet was like the sole of a calf's foot: and they sparkled like the color of burnished brass.
8) And they had the hands of a man under their wings on their four sides; and they four had their faces and their wings.
9) Their wings were joined one to another; they turned not when they went; they went every one straight forward.
10) As for the likeness of their faces, they four had the face of a man, and the face of a lion, on the right side: and they four had the face of an ox on the left side; they four also had the face of an eagle.
11) Thus were their faces: and their wings were stretched upward; two wings of every one were joined one to another, and two covered their bodies.
12) And they went every one straight forward: whither the spirit was to go, they went; and they turned not when they went.

13) As for the likeness of the living creatures, their appearance was like burning coals of fire, and like the appearance of lamps: it went up and down among the living creatures; and the fire was bright, and out of the fire went forth lightning.
14) And the living creatures ran and returned as the appearance of a flash of lightning.
15) Now as I beheld the living creatures, behold one wheel upon the earth by the living creatures, with his four faces.
16) The appearance of the wheels and their work was like unto the color of a beryl: and they four had one likeness: and their appearance and their work was as it were a wheel in the middle of a wheel.
17) When they went, they went upon their four sides: and they turned not when they went.
18) As for their rings, they were so high that they were dreadful; and their rings were full of eyes round about them four.
19) And when the living creatures went, the wheels went by them: and when the living creatures were lifted up from the earth, the wheels were lifted up.
20) Whithersoever the spirit was to go, they went, thither was their spirit to go; and the wheels were lifted up over against them: for the spirit of the living creature was in the wheels.
21) When those went, these went; and when those stood, these stood; and when those were lifted up from the earth, the wheels were lifted up over against them: for the spirit of the living creature was in the wheels. 22) And the likeness of the firmament upon the heads of the living creature was as the color of the terrible crystal, stretched forth over their heads above.
23) And under the firmament were their wings straight, the one toward the other: every one had two, which covered on this side, and every one had two, which covered on that side, their bodies.
24) And when they went, I heard the noise of their wings, like the noise of great waters, as the voice of the Almighty, the voice of speech, as the noise of an host: when they stood, they let down their wings.
25) And there was a voice from the firmament that was over their heads, when they stood, and had let down their wings.
26) And above the firmament that was over their heads was the likeness of a throne, as the appearance of a sapphire stone: and upon the likeness of the throne was the likeness as the appearance of a man above upon it.
27) And I saw as the color of amber, as the appearance of fire round about within it, from the appearance of his loins even upward and from the

appearance of his loins even downward, I saw as it were the appearance of fire, and it had brightness round about.

28) As the appearance of the bow that is in the cloud in the day of rain, so was the appearance of the brightness round about. This was the appearance of the likeness of the glory of the Lord. And when I saw it, I fell upon my face and I heard a voice of one that spake.

Let's take a closer look at verse 4. In Blumrich's view, recalling his experiences with lunar landing modules, the *cloud* mentioned by Ezekiel in verse 4 was caused by the downdraft of the vehicle during its descent. More specifically, as Blumrich explains, "Before the rocket engine can be ignited, the whole system of suction lines, pumps, etc., must be cooled down to the low temperature of liquid hydrogen in order to achieve the necessary working conditions. This is done by forcing liquid hydrogen under pressure from the tank through the system. Hydrogen is eventually discharged into the atmosphere as a very cold gas. The water contained in the air (in the form of humidity) freezes into ice crystals and becomes visible in the form of a cloud..."

The fire in verse 4 was generated by the craft's engine operation and emitted from the tail. What the King James version translates as the *colour of amber* is translated by many others as "gleaming bronze," thus making reference to the shine of a metallic surface.

In verse 5, Ezekiel describes the four shapes that he sees as coming from the midst of the cloud, which a descending craft would seem to be doing. In verses 5-7, Ezekiel sees four shapes that resemble humans, have wings, and have straight legs with round feet. Blumrich believes that the four shapes are actually four vertical cylinders with helicopter rotor above them and round flat landing pods underneath them. In other words, a single craft composed of flat landing pods, four vertical helicopter units, and a larger central control unit that holds the four vertical units together (see figures 39, 40).

In verses 8-10, in addition to wings, Ezekiel sees human hands and faces on the cylindrical objects four vertical structures. Blumrich sees the *hands* as mechanical arms, similar to the robot arms we have today (see right side of helicopter unit in figure 40). The *faces* are most likely how Ezekiel perceived the gears and control mechanisms above the rotor" of each of the four cylinders. The protrusions and configurations of these mechanisms were unknown to Ezekiel, so he just compared them to the closest known thing that popped into his mind, namely faces.

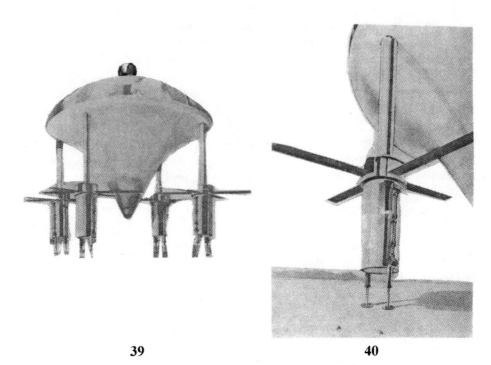

39 (Landing capsule Blumrich believes Ezekiel saw)

40 (Closeup of a helicopter unit on the capsule)

Verses 11-14 first tell of two set of rotor blades, upper and lower, on each cylinder. The upper blades are apparently folded upward in a resting position, while the lower ones are folded downward. Verse 12 describes the straight forward motion of the craft. Verses 13 and 14 are how Ezekiel perceives the illumination of the craft's central engine reactor and the flickering lights of its control rockets.

Verses 15-21 are Ezekiel's description of the well-known *wheel in the middle of a wheel* (see figure 41), which is the most often quoted aspect of Ezekiel's sighting. Blumrich considers this as the deployment of the craft's wheels for movement after it landed. He explains further that these must be retractable wheels, else they would have been visible to Ezekiel earlier and he would have included them in his description of the cylinders *arms* and *wings*. The comparison to a mineral (beryl in the King James version) is simply Ezekiel's way of indicating what color he thought the wheels were. Blumrich notes that the *wheel in the middle of a wheel* that Ezekiel refers to beginning with verse 16 is probably the way any technically untrained observer would describe it, especially in Ezekiel's era. The wheel design, in Blumrich's view, includes additional drive disks inside the outer part that rotate to cause the separate turning of the wheels. Blumrich explains that this "simultaneous rotation in several directions...creates the paradoxical illusion that there is more than one wheel in the wheel." The *eyes* were holes on the outer surface of the wheels (see the periodic indentures in the periphery of figure 41). The *spirit* referred to by Ezekiel in verses 20-21, was his way of conveying the idea that the wheels were powered by some invisible force, which he presumed emanated from the cylinders. Incidentally, this *wheel in the middle of a wheel* is the apparatus that Blumrich constructed and patented.

41

(Blumrich's structural layout of a *wheel in the middle of a wheel* device)

As Blumrich explains, each wheel rolled in various directions by rotating around a central hub while its segments (in the spaces between the spokes) rotated around separate axes. He compared the omni-directional wheel to a car tire's inner tube. Normally it rolls in one particular direction. But if twisted in itself, it will move correspondingly at a right angle to its usual direction. Combining these two directions of movement appropriately would allow the wheel to move in any direction.

Verses 22-23 describe the main body of the space craft. To many ufologists, including Blumrich, the *firmament* is a shining dome-like shape covering all four cylinders below. Blumrich narrows it further to the arched undersurface of the main part of the ship. Ezekiel likens its surface to that of a rock crystal.

In verses 24-25, Ezekiel recounts the sounds emitted by the craft. Blumrich interprets Ezekiel's statement in verse 24 that the *noise of the wings* sounded like the *noise of many waters* as an unmistakable indication that Ezekiel had heard the sounds made by the rotors as they spun. And in verse 25, the *sound from above the firmament* came from the larger central part of the ship, which was situated above all four cylinders. It then follows logically that after Ezekiel had heard what Blumrich interprets as the "idling central power plant" of the ship, the four sets of rotor blades stopped spinning and the lower ones folded downward.

What Ezekiel reports in verse 26 seems to confirm Blumrich's interpretation thus far. Ezekiel's *throne with the likeness...of a man* on it is what most people today would immediately recognize as a pilot seated in the cockpit of an aircraft.

In Blumrich's view, verse 27, which focuses on the optical effects of the different forms and brightness of light that Ezekiel saw, suggests that Ezekiel was describing a bright suit worn by the pilot. Blumrich draws this conclusion based on the fact that Ezekiel used the being's *loins* (groin-thigh area?) as point of spatial reference when describing the lights. The *amber...fire...* was above his loins (upper part of his suit?) and the *fire...brightness...* was below (the legs of the suit?). Blumrich conjectures that the suit likely had a protective metallic outer layer that reflected light.

In verse 28, Blumrich interprets the *bow* as the light reflected from the space capsule's upper outer curvature. The *...brightness round about...* refers to the light and reflections of the capsule which in which the pilot sat. From Ezekiel's perspective the brightness surrounded the pilot.

Other UFO Sightings in the Bible?

Are there other possible UFO sightings in the Bible besides Ezekiel's? This question would be easy to answer if UFOs were described in those days like we describe them today. But in the time of Ezekiel, the vocabulary used to describe any type of phenomena, including flying objects, was limited, low-tech and religiously oriented, thus very unclear to modern readers. Fowler notes that just a jew short decades ago, African Bantu tribesmen described an airplane as a "giant bird with the roar of thousands of lions." If we didn't know what the Bantus were referring to, would the picture of an airplane immediately come to mind? Perhaps, but not likely. Ezekiel's account of what had happened at the Chebar river was not only similar to the Bantu's in subjective interpretation, but also included a religious framework, reducing its objectivity even more.

One way to overcome the lack of modern objectivity is to ascertain and list the *telltale* signs of a UFO or EBE and apply these signs to a possible sighting. Such a list would include, for example, 1) devices used for flight, 2) beings or angels, often humanoid in appearance, but with special non-human qualities and 3) beings in the sky observing humans below.

I. Devices used for flight.

As noted earlier, flying and other aerial phenomena were often associated in biblical times with divinity. If a human was seen flying through the air, witnesses would assume that God was powering his flight. Likewise, if a non-human who wasn't a bird or other known aerial animal was seen flying, witnesses would likely describe it as an angel or some other divine entity. I am not saying that no one has ever flown with divine help. What I am saying is that, with or without divine help, physical alien beings and devices, both subject to the laws of physics, were probably involved in many of the unusual aerial phenomena reported in the Bible. As a matter of fact, every case of human and angelic flight mentioned in the Bible has included some type of device to aid the flights. A logical question, of course, is why devices were needed at all, if they were divine in origin. Let's review some of those devices, which include whirlwinds, clouds and chariots.

Whirlwinds are sometimes mentioned in the Bible as aerial transport vehicles. An example is 2 Kings 2:1:

> And it came to pass, when the Lord would take up Elijah into heaven by a whirlwind, that Elijah went with Elisha from Gilgal.

But was it literally a whirlwind that picked Elijah up? Was is really one of those strong rotating winds that we know to be so uncontrollable and deadly? I think not. Why would God or anyone transport Elijah in such a dangerous manner? It's much more likely that the writer used the term *whirlwind* here as the closest visual approximation of what he saw. The book of Jeremiah offers a different, more destructive view of a whirlwind. Chapter 23, verse 19 reads:

> Behold a whirlwind of the Lord is gone forth in fury, even a grievous whirlwind: it shall fall grievously upon the head of the wicked.

This was clearly some type of airborne object, as it was in Elijah's case, but one with different behavior. In the writer's view, it was intentionally sent by the Lord for a definite purpose—destruction. And since its target was Sodom and Gomorrah, which was destroyed by "fire and brimstone" and not a real whirlwind, the whirlwind in this case could conceivably have been the author's term for what we would call an explosive missile.

Habakkuk 13:3 tells of what appears to be a normal whirlwind:

> Therefore they shall be as the morning cloud, and as the early dew that passeth away, as the chaff that is driven with the whirlwind out of the floor.

So even though the term whirlwind has been used in various literal and non-literal ways, one of its basic qualities remain invariable– it always involves a flying object. And, when used in a non-natural sense, the flying object always transports either passengers or destruction towards some destination. Could we compare Elijah's whirlwind to a modern-day UFO? Quite possibly, but it's difficult to say whether the writer is using the word whirlwind for its visual or functional similarities to Elijah's vehicle. If only functionally motivated, Elijah's term could be virtually any type of UFO, since they all fly and transport passengers. If visually motivated, a whirlwind could refer to the lower cylindrical part of a whirlwind that often touches the ground and lifts any objects in its path. In this sense, Elijah's whirlwind could have been either a separate cylindrically shaped UFO or a vertical energy beam or tube of some sort that lifted him up to a waiting ship.

The latter scenario seems to be indicated at times in conjunction with another air transport device–a *chariot*. There's very little doubt that the term *chariot* indicates a flying passenger vehicle of some kind. We see in 2 Kings 2:11, an instance where Elijah is picked up and flown away by a whirlwind in the presence of a *chariot of fire*:

> And it came to pass, as they still went on, and talked, that, behold, there appeared a chariot of fire, and horses of fire, and parted them both asunder; and Elijah went up by a whirlwind into heaven.

First of all, the writer is apparently making the presence of the whirlwind secondary in importance to and therefore contingent on the presence of the chariot. Second, Elijah wasn't put into the whirlwind by someone else and he certainly didn't climb into it. He was lifted *by* the whirlwind. Thus the whirlwind in this case seems to be an airborne device that lifts Ezekiel into a hovering object that has just opened up to receive him. (Incidentally, if this did involve a UFO, it would have been a CE-4, right?) Some verses, including 2 Kings 2:1 seem to depict the whirlwind as a separate air vehicle that lifts and then flies away with the passenger. The common denominator in both passenger scenarios is that the whirlwind is an aerial transport device of some type.

Recall that in the fourth verse of Ezekiel's vision a whirlwind is briefly mentioned as along with yet another airborne object–a *cloud*, just prior to Ezekiel's description of the object that landed. Blumrich interpreted the cloud as the result of the landing craft's downdraft during its descent, which may well be true. But it's not the only possibility. The cloud could also have been another flight device or air ship. Let's examine this possibility a little closer.

The Bible frequently mentions clouds as flight devices. Of course, not every mention of a cloud refers to one. When it does, the circumstances usually make it fairly clear. The immediate question on everyone's mind, naturally, is how could someone fly aboard something so unsubstantial as a cloud? Once again, bear in mind the limited vocabulary of people in biblical times. Recall that they described events with words that reflected their own knowledge and experiences up to that point. And understand that the closest things to those objects that they had ever beheld had been clouds, which is how they described them.

The next question that surfaces is, if the objects are not really clouds, then what are they? Imagine, for a moment, how clouds look. They have almost every imaginable form, right? Let's take a quick look at some of those forms:

1) Flat like disks (stratus clouds).
2) Cloud groups, which include circular ones (cumulus, cirrocumulus and stratocumulus clouds).
3) Flat underside with arched top (altostratus and cirrostratus clouds).
4) Flat underside with raised top that forms a triangular shape (nimbostratus clouds).
5) Vertically formed and often pillar shaped (cumulonimbus clouds).
6) Oblong, cylindrical and cigar-shaped (cirrus clouds).

Do these various cloud shapes ring any bells? Do disks, spheres, cigars, triangles and cylinders remind you of the shapes of other objects that we've examined in this book? You bet they do! Many UFOs have the same forms (see cloud reference in Northwest Africa sighting earlier in this chapter). Is it just a coincidence then that many of the *clouds* that have transported men and angels through the air in the Bible have had shapes like these? Let's glance at a biblical example. Exodus 13:21-2 tells of a flying object that resembles a *pillar of a cloud* and a *pillar of fire*:

> And the Lord went before them by day in a pillar of a cloud, to lead them the way; and by night in a pillar of fire, to give them light; to go by day and night: He took not away the pillar of the cloud by day, nor the pillar of fire by night, from before the people.

First of all, who is the Lord in these verses? It's clear that the Lord referred to by Moses is whatever being or force that occupies and presumably controls the flying pillar. Why is Moses assuming that the object's occupant is divine? Is it because Moses was no different from other ancient people who often assumed that the flight of an unusual being or object indicated a divine presence? Regarding the pillar itself, it's fairly obvious that the *pillar of a cloud* and the *pillar of fire* are the same object. By day, it had the gray or silver color of many clouds and UFOs. By night it emitted a light, like many UFOs. People in those days, of course, had no concept of artificial light and thus had no word for it. For that reason, Moses might have used the closest word that he knew to the type of light that he saw: fire. Another possibility is that the color of the object really did resemble fire. Recall the many modern-era sightings that describe the color of some UFOs as fiery, particularly the color of *foo fighters*.

II. Beings or angels, humanoid in appearance but with non-human qualities.

In virtually all areas of the Bible where angels or other divine beings are mentioned, they are described as very humanoid, but sometimes with qualities that differentiate them from *normal* humans. In Genesis 18:1-3, Abraham sees beings that are clearly non-human, but that appear so human that he calls them *men* at various times:

> And the Lord appeared unto him in the plains of Mamre: and he sat in the tent door in the heat of the day. And he lift up his eyes and looked, and lo, three men stood by him: and when he saw them, he ran to meet them from the tent door, and bowed himself toward the ground, and said, My Lord, if now I have found favour in thy sight, pass not away, I pray thee, from thy servant...

These beings are obviously not humans, because Abraham connects them to the Lord whom he sees immediately prior to their appearance. But how does he know that he has just seen the Lord? How does he know how the Lord looks? In all likelihood, he saw an entity of some sort with visible characteristics that he interpreted as divine. What are some of these characteristics? Well, two immediately come to mind. First, the power of flight. Second, the emission of a bright light. Recall verse 28 of Ezekiel's vision where he ascribes divinity to a bright light. There's a distinct possibility that Abraham sees both in this case. A UFO that emits light lands near Abraham and three humanoid beings emerge from it. Why else would Abraham have just seen something that he considered the Lord and then immediately afterwards sees three non-human beings appear before him whom he also considers divine?

The 19th chapter of Genesis presents a second possibility. This case involves two beings whom Lot alternately refers to as *angels* and *men*. He invites them into his house where they eat and sleep like other humans. Question: Would real angels need to eat and sleep? Obviously, whatever they were, they were made of flesh and blood. In the 10th and 11th verses, the visitors protect Lot by blinding the attackers:

> But the men put forth their hand, and pulled Lot into the house to them, and shut the door. And they smote the men that were at the door of the house with blindness, both small and great so that they wearied themselves to find the door.

Did the visitors blind the attackers with some kind of laser device? Whatever they used, it was something that was certainly beyond the technology of that era. According to the story, these visitors warned Lot that Sodom and Gomorrah would be destroyed by what seemed like an atomic explosion. Consider verses 24, 25 and 28:

> Then the Lord rained upon Sodom and upon Gomorrah brimstone and fire from the Lord out of heaven. And he overthrew those cities, and all the plain, and all the inhabitants of the cities, and that which grew upon the ground... ((Lot)) looked toward Sodom and Gomorrah, and toward all the land of the plain, and beheld, and, lo, the smoke of the country went up as the smoke of a furnace.

Is the fire that rained upon Sodom and Gomorrah a missile or bomb? Isn't the total devastation described by the author reminiscent of Hiroshima and Nagasaki? Doesn't the *smoke* of this explosion remind you of the mushroom cloud created by an atomic bomb?

So we see two flesh-and-blood humanoid beings whom Lot considers angels. They look human, but possess non-human abilities (device that blinds). They've come to warn Lot of the impending destruction of Sodom and Gomorrah by what appears to be an atomic explosion. In my view, a reasonable assumption is that these were alien beings sent by others like them to warn Lot of the destruction of a city that had become very depraved and perverse.

The inevitable question is why extraterrestrials would want to destroy a corrupted earthly city. If my assumption is correct, the answer would most likely be connected to alien intervention in our genetic development, which we will discuss more in chapter 8. Perhaps their intervention included safeguarding their genetic handiwork. That is, ensuring that no undesirable genetic strains or mutations occurred. It is clear that many residents of Sodom and Gomorrah practiced acts that were considered deviant, most notably homosexuality. But could they have become genetically polluted by homosexual acts? Of course not. But some researchers suspect that they went beyond homosexuality. Way beyond. I've read translations of ancient documents that report sexual acts as deviant as bestiality in some places, including Sodom and Gomorrah. If those reports are correct, genetic pollution could indeed have occurred, because mankind was said to be at a phase in the genetic intervention process when humans and lower species of animals could produce offspring together. Those same documents allege that many of the old myths and pictures that show human-animal hybrid creatures were therefore to be taken literally. At this point, let me make it clear that this information is more speculative than confirmed. I'm just mentioning it as a possible motivation for the destruction of Sodom and Gomorrah. Further comment on it is beyond the scope of this book, so, I'll drop it for now and perhaps revisit it in a future book.

III. Beings in the sky observing humans below.

If these biblical reports are really about UFOs, they would be consistent with our present facts about UFO activity. But much has changed since then regarding our relationship with extraterrestrials, especially in relation to direct contact with them. This contact has gradually diminished, and understandably so, given the long span of time since the era of alien genetic intervention. In chapter 8, I'll detail why I think modern man is the result of alien genetic intervention that occurred millenia ago. For now, suffice it to say that if intervention is still occurring, it no longer involves the whole of mankind as it once did, but possibly isolated cases (such as the alleged experiences reported by some UFO abductees). In other words, after the aliens had finished the main part of their genetic work with us, their chief concern switched from the close and constant contact of large-scale intervention to more distant contact involving mostly checks on the progress of their handiwork.

These alien checks on our progress appear to be the aspect of their relationship with us that has changed the least through the centuries and millenia. As we read earlier, EBEs, in their guardian roles, are still observing and checking on us. From a human perspective, the main difference between ancient times and today is that, when we sight a UFO overhead now, we'll wonder what it is and why it's there. In ancient times, as we examined in the section on mythology, many groups were well aware of and comfortable with the constant hovering presence of alien vessels. Does the Bible have anything to say about such observers? It sure seems to. Let's take a look at some of King Nebuchadnezzar's second dream in Daniel 4:13:

> I saw in the visions of my head upon my bed, and behold a *watcher* and an holy one came down from heaven.

Who is this watcher? It seems to be an entity in the sky whose function it is to observe. Note how the verse differentiates between the watcher and a divine being. It would thus seem that the divine being is an entity whose presence is special, while the watcher is one whose presence is more of a common occurrence. What kind of an entity can hover in the skies for so long that it becomes commonplace? Were the watchers UFOs?

So, have our discussions on the telltale signs of UFOs and EBEs made us any more certain of whether or not the Bible verses we've read really involve extraterrestrials? For some of us, perhaps, and for others, perhaps not, depending on how open-minded you and how you interpret and apply these and other telltale signs. As for my own opinion, the extraterrestrial explanation sounds much more plausible than many that I've heard thus far. Most other interpretations tend to produce more questions than answers.

Would UFOs Contradict the Bible?

What if the beings and devices in those Bible verses are conclusively proven to be EBEs and UFOs? Would they then be viewed as contradictions to biblical teachings and principles? I say they wouldn't. I say the reality of UFOs is just as compatible with the Bible as it is with the holy scriptures of several other religions and belief systems. Many Old Testament readers will insist that if UFOs and EBEs ever existed they must have been demonic in origin, because extraterrestrials are not mentioned by name there. With all due respect for such opinions, it seems a bit unreasonable to say that something that is not mentioned in the Bible has to be evil. According to this logic, I could say that ferrets are satanic beasts, right?

Then there are those who ask what role God could have possibly given to extraterrestrials if they exist. A good question, and fairly easy to answer. At least as easy as the question of what role God gave to Africans, or Asians, or Europeans, or any other ethnic group or culture indigenous to the Earth. Why can't EBEs have the same basic God-given roles vis-a-vis the human race as our various earthly groups have vis-a-vis one another? It's generally assumed that when God wants to intervene among humans, He rarely does so directly, but rather indirectly, through material beings like ourselves. Why not also through EBEs? Why can't EBEs also have divine missions and callings in life? Isn't it possible that EBEs have been used by God to bring civilization to the primitive beings that used to be our ancestors before they inexplicably became modern almost overnight? Couldn't God have allowed them to intervene genetically, in order to give us the mental capacity to take that step up toward civilization, and then to train us? We can draw somewhat of an analogy between this and the situation in which Europeans came to the new world and conquered the native Americans there. Subsequently, the conquerors taught them the ways of civilization and their missionaries brought them modern religion, which many religious people still claim was in God's will. After all, they say, if the Europeans had not *intervened*, the natives would have never become civilized and thus would have never known about the *real* God. Thus, according to many people, God used the conquerors to carry out His will. Couldn't this reasoning be applied to the role of extraterrestrials? Couldn't they also be considered as *civilizers* and missionaries?

James Edward Gilmer

If the human race survives long enough it will one day launch manned missions to other planets and solar systems, just as our extraterrestrial neighbors did. While colonizing other worlds, which is inevitable, what would we do if we encountered primitive species of humanoids? Species similar to our ancestors before we became *modern*. Correct! We'd do the same thing that we'd do on Earth with uncivilized native tribes. We'd civilize them. And if we thought it necessary, we'd intervene genetically (we're already intervening genetically with plants and lower animal species, right?). Wouldn't we consider it divinely justified to *help* species on other worlds in this manner? Is the idea of EBEs doing the same with us really any different?

Chapter 6

Where Do UFOs Go?

One of the most baffling questions about UFOs is where they go after a sighting. The answer would undoubtedly also tell us where they are based. There are numerous, sometimes widely diverging views on this, ranging from supernatural locations to more mundane ones. Let's take a quick glance at a few of them:

Interdimensional Travel?

Some claim to have seen UFOs materialize and dematerialize as a result of inter-dimensional travel. This would mean, among other things, that UFOs come from dimensional configurations that are different from ours. For example, their space-time fabric could contain more than the three spatial dimensions present in ours. They are said to materialize into our world when their configurations are shifted to match ours and to de-materialize when they're shifted back the other way.

Others suggest that UFOs might materialize from the plane of existence that some of us think of as *bardo* or the spirit world. Thus, UFOs would share the same dimensional environment as supernatural entities that we sometimes think of as ghosts and demons. According to this notion, UFOs materialize into our world in the same manner that ghostly apparitions do. Both are said to have access to a type of interdimensional window.

Black Holes, White Holes and Wormholes?

There are those who propose that UFOs fly away to parallel universes through *wormholes*. A wormhole is a theoretical conduit or tunnel through the space-time fabric of our known universe. Some cosmologists theorize that the entrance to such a tunnel is opened by a *black hole*, which is what remains of a red supergiant star that has supernovaed and left behind a core so massive that it collapses on itself and becomes so dense that its enormous gravitational pull requires an escape velocity greater than the speed of light. In other words, this massive core collapses into a dense point called a *singularity*, that forms an *event horizon* around itself, a gravitational field so strong that nothing entering it, not even light, can escape its grasp.

A popular theory of black holes is that they are static, meaning they don't rotate. According to this view, any solid object, like a space ship or a human body would be crushed into oblivion when sucked into the singularity at the core. Other theories that are apparently gaining steam are that black holes may be 1) electrically charged and 2) not static but, like most other large celestial bodies, including whole galaxies and maybe our entire Universe itself, rotate. If they are electrically charged and/or rotate, then they might have a second event horizon inside. Simply put, such an inner event horizon could mean that space-time, which changed at the outer event horizon changes again at the inner one. This, in turn, could mean that a solid body wouldn't meet the same catastrophic fate as it would within a static black hole.

If a space ship could enter a black hole and remain intact, some theorists say that it could continue on through and resurface elsewhere through another space-time warping aperture–a *white hole*. While a black hole is seen as an implosion, a white hole is seen as a complementary explosion. That is, what a black hole sucks in, a white hole spews out. The black hole is the entrance and the white hole is the exit. If black and white holes are indeed paired in this manner, many astronomers believe that the connection pathway between them–*wormholes*–could be used as interstellar expressways to other solar systems, galaxies and maybe even other universes. (Stuttman, vol.3)

Closer to Home

As appealing as such scenarios might sound, I prefer a different one, one that appears much more likely to be true. Yes, I agree that, given the reality of things like UFOs, black holes and possibly white holes and wormholes, other fantastic notions like inter-dimensional travel should not be dismissed from the realms of the conceivable. But, as I'm sure you can tell by now, I'm more inclined to support theories and aspects of UFOs for which clear concrete evidence exists. Evidence at least as convincing as what I've presented for the existence and behavior of UFOs thus far. The theories and claims of interdimensional and wormhole travel lack such corroboration and are totally speculative. Regarding a spiritual dimension, although I am certain of its reality, I don't buy into the notion that it serves as a base of any kind for UFOs.

The bulk of the evidence that I've examined thus far points more convincingly to our own universe as the sole place of origin and to our own solar system as the present location of bases for the UFOs that have been visiting us. In other words, most information and evidence on UFOs, including what we've examined thus far in this book, clearly indicates that UFOs and their bases are part of our physical reality and that when UFOs fly away after a sighting, they go no further than the boundaries of our own solar system.

Which Planets and Moons?

Assuming now that UFOs do fly to locations within our solar system, we should focus our discussion on those areas where physical bases are most likely established; namely planets and moons. But which ones? Well, first of all, judging by their long history of visits to our air spaces and their apparent tolerance of terrestrial environmental conditions, it would be safe to assume that UFOs bases are somewhere nearby. Nearby meaning somewhere within what is considered the habitable zone of our solar system; the region comprising the orbits of Venus, Earth and Mars. Of course, beings as advanced as our extraterrestrial visitors might have the technology to inhabit environments that we consider uninhabitable. So, we should bear this in mind when considering the friendliness or unfriendliness of other planets. Let's take a quick glance at the possibilities.

The Jovian Planets

The planets in our solar system are generally categorized as inner or outer planets; that is, planets having orbits either inside or outside that of the asteroid belt.

42

The inner planets are called terrestrial, because they exhibit qualities similar to those of earth. The outer planets are called jovian (except for the anomalous Pluto, which many scientists consider technically neither jovian nor terrestrial) because they exhibit qualities similar to those of the largest planet in our solar system, Jupiter (figure 42). And, of course, Jove is another Latin name for Jupiter, the Roman version of Zeus, the supreme god of Greek mythology. The other jovian planets are Saturn, Uranus and Neptune. Besides the fact that they're outer planets, jovian planets differ from terrestrial ones in several other ways. Among them, they are larger, they rotate faster, their orbits are longer, they have rings and thick atmospheres, and each jovian has several moons.

It is other differences, however, that make jovian planets less humanoid-friendly than terrestrial planets. The most noticeable difference is surface consistency. While terrestrial planets have solid surfaces, jovians don't. They are generally characterized as gas giants, meaning that, like the sun, they consist of mainly hydrogen, helium, and smaller amounts of other elements, instead of the rocky and metallic materials that make up terrestrials. Some of the other gaseous elements of jovians are the cloud layers of ammonia ice and ammonium hydrosulfide ice on Jupiter and Saturn, and the significant levels of methane on Uranus and Neptune. Regarding their gaseous composition, jovian atmospheres never really end, they simply become denser at deeper levels because of the high pressures. These pressures eventually convert the hydrogen gas into hot liquid form at lower depths. Even the so-called rocky cores of jovians have this liquid consistency. No signs of present or previous life have been found thus far on the jovian planets.

Jovian Moons

Of the 60 plus known moons that orbit the outer planets, Europa, and Titan are considered by many astronomers to contain more life-sustaining conditions than the others. Europa, one of Jupiter's 16 moons, is said to possibly have a sea of liquid water beneath what appears to be a crust of water ice. Liquid water, of course, is necessary for life on earth. Europa, however, may be too cold to suit humanoid life, with an average temperature that is only about 43 percent of the Earth's average of about 60 degrees Fahrenheit. This means that Europa's temperature is consistently below freezing. Furthermore, Europa has an extremely thin atmosphere, with a pressure that is only about a billionth of the Earth's. Titan is one of Saturn's moons and the second largest moon in our solar system after Jupiter's Ganymede. It is bitterly cold with an icy surface. What distinguishes Titan as a possible life sustainer is that its atmosphere is thick with the organic molecules carbon monoxide, nitrogen compounds, and various hydrocarbons. The predominant gas in its atmosphere, nitrogen (97%), also predominates in earth's atmosphere (78%). The most inhospitable aspect of this moon is that it may have large bodies of liquid methane or ethane. As with the jovian planets, no signs of life have yet been detected on these or any other jovian moons.

The Terrestrial Planets

As mentioned above, the terrestrial planets are the inner planets, those that orbit the sun inside the orbit of the asteroid belt. Unlike the gas giants, they are solid and composed of mainly rocky and metallic substances. Unfortunately, just their solid composition alone doesn't make the other terrestrial planets as humanoid friendly as Earth. As a matter of fact, two of them, Mercury and Venus, appear to be very inhospitable. Mercury, the smallest of the inner planets and the closest to the sun, has no water and virtually no atmosphere, which are features generally associated with planetary life support. The lack of an atmosphere also exposes Mercury to potentially heavy doses of such things as ultraviolet radiation, meteoroid showers, and X-rays–things which are extremely detrimental to life forms. Without an atmosphere, Mercury also experiences extreme temperature swings. When it's dark, the temperature dips to well below freezing, while in the daylight it climbs to a sizzling 800 degrees fahrenheit.

Venus is the second terrestrial planet from the sun and is sometimes called earth's sister planet, because it is closer to the Earth than other planets in size, mass, and distance (figure 43). But the favorable comparisons end there. Venus has no water and a very unfriendly atmosphere for humanoids and other life forms. Its atmosphere is composed of over 96 % carbon dioxide, which combines with hot sulfur molecules that seep out of surface rocks to foster a runaway greenhouse effect, resulting in hellish surface temperatures of about 900 degrees fahrenheit. This scorching heat has caused any water that may have been on Venus to evaporate. This atmosphere is made even more stifling and corrosive by dense layers of sulfuric acid clouds and rain believed by many scientists to result from the release of sulfur dioxide gas from Venus's ongoing volcanic activity. If a life form somehow manages to survive the searing heat and choking carbon dioxide, it would have to contend with crushing surface pressures of up to 90 Earth atmospheres!

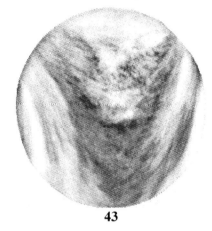
43

Interestingly enough, though, the fact that, besides carbon dioxide, the remainder of the atmosphere is mostly nitrogen, means that organic gases predominate in the Venusian atmosphere. That, plus the fact that the extreme greenhouse effect wasn't always present, lends some credence to those who insist that a civilization once existed on Venus. Scientists generally concede that surface conditions on Venus were indeed once much more life-friendly than they are now. Many even speculate that the surface probably once hosted dense jungle life. So, who knows? Maybe some of our extraterrestrial neighbors originated on Venus and left when it became uninhabitable.

The Habitable Zone

Again, the habitable zone is the orbital area that theoretically provides the best chance for the development of conditions that promote and sustain life. This is because water, a key ingredient in the development and maintenance of life, can theoretically be liquid on the planet's surface. The celestial bodies in this zone are those in the immediate vicinity of Earth, Mars, and Venus. We already know that Venus has no liquid water, so let's examine the other possibilities–our Moon and Mars.

The Enigmatic Moon

The Moon's Origin

44

Earth's closest celestial neighbor, the Moon (figure 44), has become quite an enigma for the scientific community over the past thirty years. Much of what we previously thought we knew about our lunar satellite no longer holds true, and new discoveries have raised more questions than they've answered. For example, the prevailing theories about the Moon's origin have recently been either discarded or seriously weakened. David Childress (1994) recalls one theory that held that the Moon might have formed from the same cloud of cosmic dust and gases that produced the Earth about 4.6 billion years ago. But now we know that this was incorrect, since nearly 100 percent of Moon rocks analyzed thus far have been found to be older than at least 90 percent of the oldest rocks on earth. Another theory proposed that the Moon could be a section of the earth torn away millions of years ago by some cosmic cataclysm. This notion has also been dismissed, because we now know that the Earth's composition differs significantly from that of the Moon. A theory that still has some popularity suggests that the Moon was passing by the earth and was "captured" by its gravitational field. Most scientists now maintain, however, that the dynamics required for such a capture would have made it nearly impossible for it to have occurred between the Earth and the Moon. For one thing, the Moon is too large to have been captured by the Earth in such a manner.

A more recent theory, as Jim Marrs (1997) points out, was that the Moon formed from space debris left over from the Earth's creation. This too has now been dismissed due to the gravitational principle that states that a large body will attract all loose material leaving none to form a smaller body. The most popular theory among astronomers at present is that a collision between the Earth and another celestial body gave birth to the Moon about 4.6 billion years ago. According to this view, the other body shattered into many pieces, went into orbit around the Earth and then gradually came together again as the Moon. However, the scientific community acknowledges that this theory has the obvious inherent weakness that no space debris from such a collision has ever been detected.

A Watery Moon?

It was back in 1994 when NASA first developed serious suspicions that the Moon contained water. That was when a probe it had launched, the Clementine, had received a radar signal that indicated the presence of hydrogen at the Moon's south pole, suggesting that ice was in the area. In 1998, the Lunar Prospector confirmed NASA's suspicions during its mission to the Moon. It detected hydrogen in what turned out to be significant amounts of frozen water at both lunar poles. Significant in this case meaning amounts in the neighborhood of several billion tons of ice at each pole. Regarding the origin of the water, most scientists propose that it was delivered as ice by billions of years of bombardment by meteorites and comets, which, of course, implies that the original source of the water was totally external. Such an implication is misleading, to say the least, because, intentionally or unintentionally, it conceals other evidence that indicates that lunar water may have another source–the interior of the Moon!

You heard correctly. The interior of the Moon. And not just water ice, but also liquid ice. What evidence exists for such a notion? Well, consider what happened following the Apollo 15 mission. Childress noted that NASA scientists had detected upwards of 100 square miles of water vapor wafting above the Moon's surface over a 14-hour period. Scrambling to devise some explanation that would help them preserve their theory about surface water ice, they proceeded to offer a number of reasons, each of which was quickly shot down for lack of plausibility. Finally, NASA conceded that the water vapor probably came from inside the Moon and acknowledged the fact that astronomers had reported seeing such vapor clouds hanging above the lunar surface on several previous occasions. If the vapor didn't come from the interior, then it would have to be some thin layer of atmospheric clouds. That, of course, is impossible, because the Moon's gravitational field (one-sixth that of the earth) is too weak to hold such atmospheric phenomena in its grasp.

James Edward Gilmer

A Hollow Moon?

According to prevailing scientific theory, the Moon is basically a solid body composed of various layers. First, a solid crust below the dusty regolith (surface) estimated to be about 50 miles deep, give or take 10 miles. Then a mantle, which, like the crust, is composed mainly of solid rock. Finally, a core, also solid. Thus, it is said to have a structure similar to that of the Earth, although the Earth, being much larger than the Moon, comprises multiple layers of each type. It's a neat theory and sounds plausible enough to be accepted by most of the scientific community, but it also has a major flaw. A flaw so major, in fact, that scientists have swept it under the rug and are trying to keep it there, so that no one notices and starts asking questions. The flaw is that the currently accepted theory of the Moon's structure fails to take into account clear evidence suggesting that the moon may actually be more hollow than solid!

More hollow than solid? Yes, it now appears to be a distinct possibility! One that NASA scientists are certainly aware of, but have generally gone to great lengths to kept mum about. According to Marrs, one NASA scientist, Dr. Gordon McDonald, was bold enough to voice such a possibility back in the 1960s. He pointed out that the Moon's interior was likely much less dense than its exterior and added that "...it would seem that the Moon is more like a hollow than a homogeneous sphere." Dr. McDonald's theory was given an unexpected boost during the Apollo 11 and 12 Moon flights. On each occasion, after the crew returned to the ship, the heavy lunar module ascent stage crashed back down onto the Moon, creating artificial moonquakes that were to be measured by ultrasensitive seismic equipment placed at the original landing sites. Astonishingly, instead of creating *regular* quaking vibrations, the crashes caused the moon to "ring like a gong or a bell, according to NASA.

The experiment carried out by Apollo 12 was especially astounding, because the Moon reverberated like a bell for over an hour. During a press conference, after word of the bizarre ringing had leaked, Maurice Ewing, one of the experiment's directors, admitted that the crash had caused the Moon to ring like a church bell and that NASA had no explanation for it. As Marrs notes, M.I.T.'s Dr. Sean Solomon had an explanation for the ringing: "The Lunar Orbiter experiments...vastly improved our knowledge of the Moon's gravitational field...indicating the frightening possibility that the Moon might be hollow."

Another possible explanation for why the Moon rang like a bell is that the specific locations struck by the lunar modules were very cavernous below the surface. Nobel Chemist Dr. Harold Urey suggested as much when commenting on the interior of the Moon, stating that it was possible that "...there is either matter much less dense than the rest of the Moon or simply a cavity." Whether cavernous or hollow, however, the puzzling fact remains that, although NASA scientists have demonstrated through repeated experiments that one or the other has to be true, neither is mentioned in our text books as possibilities. Why?

The great British astronomer, Dr. H.P. Wilkins also believes that the Moon could have a very cavernous interior. He suggested that surface "plugholes" might lead to subsurface spaces. He discovered such a plughole, nicknamed "the Washbowl", which is a large circular opening about 600 feet in diameter and situated inside a one and a half mile crater. Such openings could provide UFOs access points to and from the Moon's interior. Thus, Wilkins and other researchers point to the Moon's apparent hollow or cavernous interior and to the plugholes as strongly suggestive that UFOs have underground bases there!

Artificial Structures on the Moon?

Alien Lunar Obelisks?

NASA's lunar missions have found groups of structures that some observers, including Childress, believe were artificially constructed. One of these is a group of obelisks (see NASA photo in figure 45), called the "Blair Cuspids." It was first noticed in a photo of the Sea of Tranquility taken by the Lunar Orbiter 2 in 1996. Dr. William Blair of the Boeing Institute of Biotechnology had found that within this group of several tall pointed obelisks, some as high as a fifteen-story building, formed a system composed of six triangles and two axes pointed with obelisks. Blair dismissed the counter-arguments of those who called the structures the result of natural geophysical processes. He maintained that if they were entirely natural, they would have been distributed in a more random arrangement and not in such precise geometrical patterns. Russian Space Engineer Alexander Abramov reportedly took Blair's observation a step further and declared that the positioning of the obelisks closely resembled that of the Egyptian pyramids near Cairo, and that the central obelisks are arranged in exactly the same manner as the three great pyramids at Giza! Speaking of pyramids, there is an unusual formation of pyramid-like structures in the region of the Moon called Mare Imbrium inside a crater called Aristillus.

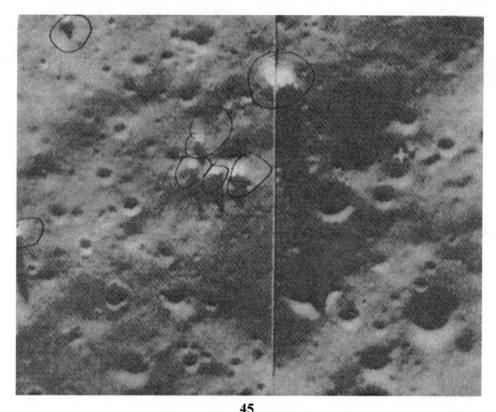

45

(The encircled lunar structures are believed by many ufologists to be artifically constructed obelisks)

A Lunar Bridge?

Another unnatural structure on the Moon is what appears to be a twelve-mile long bridge straddling the Sea of Crisis crater. Many well-known astronomers have seen it, including Dr. Wilkins and Patrick Moore of the British Astronomical Association. Dr. Wilkens stated that the structure looked artificial and that he seriously doubted that it could have formed naturally. Moore said that the bridge-like structure was a relatively recent addition to the lunar surface and seemed to have appeared there almost overnight.

The Tower?

An even more puzzling structure is one called the "Tower." Marrs recalls that an independent geologist named Dr. Bruce Cornet had studied the object in

Lunar Orbiter photographs and described it as being "...an enigma of the highest magnitude, because it rises more than five miles above the surface of the moon, and has been photographed from five different angles and two different altitudes. In all four photographs the same structure is visible and can be viewed from two different sides...The top of the Tower has a very cubic geometry and appears to be composed of regular cubes joined together to form a very large cube with an estimated width of over one mile!"

Lunar Domes?

There are many other structures on the Moon that appear to have been artificially constructed, including some that apparently suggest a UFO base on the surface of the Moon. These are the groups of so-called *domes* that dot various regions there (see NASA photos in figures 46, 47). Childress notes science writer Joseph Goodavage's description of them: "In the past few years more than 200 white, dome-shaped structures have been observed on the Moon and catalogued, but for some strange reason, they often vanish from one place and reappear somewhere else." Those who dismiss the domes as natural formations, concede that they would be ideal for protection against the increased hazards associated with the thin atmosphere of the Moon, including damage from meteors and comets. But what if aliens built them for that very reason?

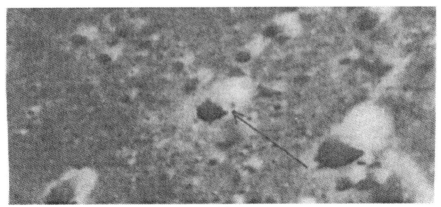

46

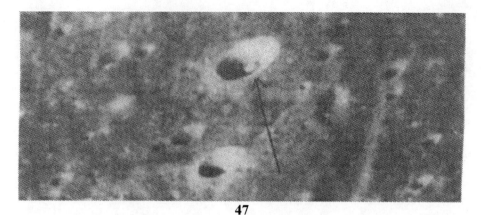

47

(The arrows in figures 46 and 47 point to what many ufologists believe are artificially constructed domes within lunar craters)

Witnesses?

Has anyone ever claimed to actually witness alien activity on the Moon? As a matter of fact, yes. According to noted UFO researcher and author Timothy Good, astronaut Neil Armstrong (figure 48) made such a claim at a NASA symposium saying, "It was incredible...the fact is, we were warned off. There was never any question then of a space station or a moon city...I can't go into any details, except to say that their ships were far superior to ours both in size and technology–boy, were they big!...and menacing." Armstrong reportedly also explained that manned landings on the Moon had ended with the Apollo missions because of the alien presence there. In this regard, he was quoted as saying that

48

"NASA...couldn't risk a panic on Earth." Good also noted that Armstrong subsequently denied making these statements.

A Strong Possibility

It's clear now that things are occurring on the Moon that our government, scientists and educators either don't know about or don't want to divulge. They are very secretive about the artificial surface structures and the Moon's cavernous if not hollow interior. And then there's the inescapable fact that our astronauts actually claim to have seen alien activity on the Moon, which NASA is officially denying. If you add all this together, even a strongly skeptical mind would have to at least concede the possibility that aliens have bases on and inside the Moon.

What About Mars?

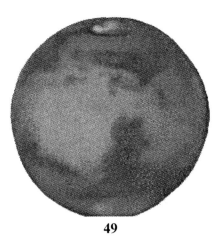

49

Mars (figure 49) has long been thought of in our popular imagination as a planet inhabited by humanoid beings. Many believe that Mars is the only other planet in our solar system that contains life, a fact reflected in the entertainment world. For example, the famous *War of the Worlds* of the 1930s was about an invasion of creatures from Mars. There was also the 1960s hit television series *My Favorite Martian,* as well as Mars-related shows and movies. As a matter of fact, we often use the words *Extraterrestrial* and *Martian* synonymously. But is this popular assumption correct? Does Mars exhibit enough life-friendly conditions to warrant its label as a possibly inhabited, or once inhabited planet? Let's examine some of its features and see.

Similarities to Earth

- Besides Earth, Mars is the only other terrestrial planet that has a moon. Actually it has two of them, Diemos and Phobos.
- Mars once had an atmosphere similar to the Earth's. The atmosphere and barometric pressure on Mars are now very thin and the atmosphere is now composed of about 95 percent carbon dioxide. Nonetheless, noticeable similarities remain; namely, small amounts of nitrogen, oxygen, and water vapor in the Martian atmosphere, which are also present in Earth's.
- The Martian poles are ice-capped like the Earth's. And, although the ice in the Martian South Pole is mainly composed of carbon dioxide, the Martian North Pole, like the Earth's is mainly water ice.

- Surface features on Mars, such as long channels, canyons, grooves, crater erosion, and other things, indicate that it once had oceans, rivers, and streams, like Earth's.
- NASA's Mars Global Surveyor recently produced images that strongly suggest that liquid water presently flows near or even on the surface of Mars! These images include such features as gullies, and deposits of soil and rock that have been recently moved by water flows.
- In 1984, scientists declared that a meteorite discovered in Antarctica had originated on Mars and possibly contained traces of microscopic fossils that had most likely been produced by living bacteria. This means, of course, that these scientists were saying that Mars once supported some form of life.
- Although the average temperature on Mars is much lower than on Earth, summer temperatures in the southern hemisphere can climb to about 70 degrees Fahrenheit.
- The large amounts of iron oxide on Mars make the rocky red surface resemble several red-soiled areas on Earth.
- The general landscape on Mars resembles that of New Mexico.
- Mars's orbital axis is inclined at 25.2 degrees, which is very close to Earth's incline of 23.5 degrees. Mars's incline also produces Earth-like seasons of the Martian year.
- Mars rotates on its axis once every 24.6 hours, nearly identical to Earth's 24-hour day.

An Alien Base on Mars?

As we have just seen, Mars has a lot of Earth-like characteristics, certainly more than the Moon does. And since we've already seen evidence strongly suggestive of an alien presence on the Moon, it would stand to reason that Mars might also be used as a base. Some people even believe that Mars was once a thriving populated planet, like Earth, and that some huge disaster, possibly a gigantic asteroid, destroyed its atmosphere, forcing the inhabitants to leave the surface. But is there any proof that any intelligent life was ever on Mars? Are there structures on Mars, like those on the Moon, that appear to have been built by intelligent beings? Absolutely! There are structures on Mars that are even more startling than those on the Moon. Let's take a look at a few of them.

Pyramidal Structures

As on the Moon, structures have been discovered on Mars that many observers insist were artificially constructed. For example, in 1971, during the Mariner 9 mission, NASA photos showed precisely formed pyramids in the area of the Elysium Quadrangle. What's more, these pyramids are enormous, reaching up to a half mile high. And like the structures on the Moon, many observers say that these Martian pyramids are too well-formed to have been created naturally.

A Space Port?

Noted science author Brian Crowley described what appeared to be some type of port for airships or spaceships on Mars. He says that "it looks for all the world like a giant airport (or space port) with a central hub and wheel-like extensions, just like a modern airport..." This configuration was photographed by both NASA's Viking and the Soviet Phobos space missions and is situated near what appears to be a large pyramid at the edge of a crater. It also bears a striking resemblance to the famous ancient Nazca lines in Peru, which are also thought to be guide markings for incoming aircraft. The patterns of the Nazca lines are nearly impossible to discern from near ground level, but become crystal clear far above the Earth's surface.

Egyptian Pyramids and Sphinx in Cydonia?

The publications of several UFO researchers and science writers, including Richard Hoagland, Mark Carlotto, David Childress, Vincent DiPietro and Gregory Molenaar, have widely publicized shocking revelations about a region of Mars called Cydonia. NASA photos from its 1976 Viking probe showed clearly-formed structures with unmistakable similarities to ancient Egyptian structures. First, perfectly formed pyramids dot the area, arranged in a manner virtually identical to that of the Egyptian pyramids in the Valley of the Kings (see NASA photo in figure 50). Second, there seems to be a modified version of the Egyptian Sphinx near the pyramids–a giant face carved in stone (see figure 51)! Third, the Cydonia Face appears to be wearing an Egyptian headdress!

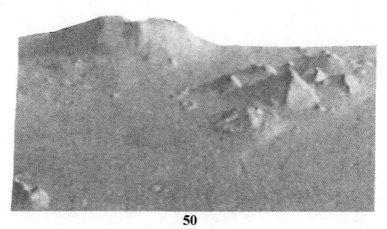

50

(Note the Mars face at the bottom left and the pyramids at the upper right in Cydonia)

The Mars Face

According to Childress, the Cydonia Face seems to have been carved out of a mountain (see NASA photo in figure 51). It's about 1.6 miles long from crown to chin, approximately 1.2 miles wide, and somewhere in the vicinity of 2000 feet high. Molenaar and DiPietro used photo enhancement techniques to show clear eye socket and eyeball details on the face, while Carlotto made enhancements that showed teeth inside its mouth!

Chariots of Gods or Demons?
The Incredible Truth About UFOs and Extraterrestrials

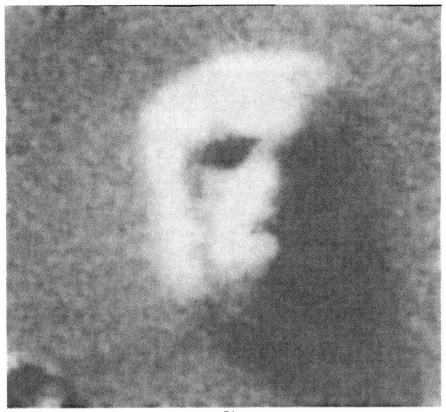

51
(A closeup of the Mars Face)

A Face in Utopia?

Childress recently brought to light evidence of at least one more face carved in Martian stone. He pointed to research done by DiPietro and Molenaar in the Utopia region in which they discovered a face with most of the features of the Cydonia Face. In addition to the same general contours, it clearly exhibits both eye cavities and an Egyptian-style headdress. Other similarities to the Cydonia Face include small indentations on both cheeks and over the right eye. Some of the features, such as the eyes, appear to have been damaged and aren't in the near perfect condition of the Cydonia Face. Nonetheless, the Utopia Face is still clearly a sculpted visage in convincing condition. Many observers maintain that too many things have to fall into place for either face to have been formed naturally, and even more for both faces to exhibit virtually identical features and markings!

James Edward Gilmer

An Underground Base?

We have now seen evidence of artificial structures on the Martian surface, even a possible landing port, but where are the UFO bases? The answer: Underground. If this is correct, it signals a definite pattern regarding the location of UFO bases. Even though we've also seen evidence of a surface base on the Moon, there appear to be underground bases in both places. We've seen an example of this on the Moon, but what about on Mars? Is there any proof of a possible UFO base below the Martian surface? Definitely! Childress recalls that, in 1989, the Russian space probe Phobos 2 took infrared photos of an area near the Martian equator that showed a huge cavernous region below the surface that seemed to be artificially shaped. It was an extensive system of large, clearly delineated rectangular spaces positioned along arrow-straight parallel lines; an arrangement that closely resembled the layout of a city on Earth! Dr. John Becklake of the London Science Museum said of this area: "The city-like pattern is 60 kilometers wide and could easily be mistaken for an aerial view of Los Angeles."

Infrared photographic equipment produces images via the heat radiating from the object. The surface of the same Martian region was also photographed using regular equipment, and nothing other than red soil and rocks showed up on the film! This means beyond a shadow of any doubt that what the infrared camera photographed was underground at the time.

Earth: The Model Terrestrial Planet

52

It goes without saying that Earth (figure 52) is the model terrestrial planet. After all, the degree of *terrestriality* of other planets is determined by how similar their conditions are to those on Earth. Our temperature, atmosphere, ecological balance, natural resources, etc., are optimal for the development and support of an almost endless number of life forms. Therefore, if beings that frequently visit us have bases on our habitable-zone neighbors, i.e. the Moon and Mars, wouldn't it make sense for them to also have bases on the most life-friendly body in our solar system–Earth? Of course, if we accept the possibility of UFO bases on Earth, they would have to be underground, as they are on Mars and the Moon, since aliens would presumably want to conceal their bases from the dangers posed by billions of naturally xenophobic Earthlings. After observing us for thousands of years, I'm sure aliens know by now that what Earthlings don't understand they fear, and what they fear they try to destroy. Besides that, underground UFO bases on Earth would be consistent with the pattern that we've already seen on the Moon and Mars. But where are these subterranean bases? And where are their access points? Both may be nearer than you think! Let's examine the possibilities in the following chapter.

Chapter 7

The Intraterrestrials

Yes, the title is right. If the aliens that have been visiting us have maintained bases below the surface of our planet for millenia, then it may be more correct to call them *intraterrestrials* than extraterrestrials! So where are they? Where are their access points? Do you remember the geographic regions on Earth where UFOs are seen the most (mountains, valleys, forests, polar regions, and large bodies of water)? Those are the main access points! They offer the best cover for the openings that aliens have identified or created that lead to deep underground caverns, tunnels, and other spaces. Like the *plugholes* on the Moon, remember? But, of course, the Moon doesn't offer as many of these types of natural cover features as the Earth does.

Can Aliens Dig Underground Without Being Discovered?

Can aliens really dig out huge subterranean areas without our knowledge? Sure they can! A reasonable question is how aliens could dig out underground bases without drawing attention to themselves with the all the noise of drilling and blasting. It's simple. They did it quietly. Consider this: Although Earthlings still use a lot of noisy and messy equipment and explosives to dig and hollow out natural areas, we also have *quiet* equipment for such jobs.

An example of such quiet equipment was noted by Erich von Daeniken (1973). Scientists at our atomic research laboratory in Los Alamos developed a *thermal drill* back in the 1970s. The drill, tipped with wolfram and heated by a graphite heating element, bores into the earth by melting rocks, as the name implies, instead of blowing them up. The German magazine *Der Spiegel* reported that the initial test model bored quickly and nearly soundlessly through 12 ft thick blocks of stone. Because of the success of the first model, plans were quickly drawn up to develop larger, nuclear-powered versions of the thermal drill, with the long-term goal of penetrating deep into the Earth's crust. My point, of course, is that, if we have the technology to dig quickly and noiselessly with thermal drills, shouldn't we assume that our alien neighbors have the technology to dig even faster and more quietly? And even in the areas where we've drilled, we've barely scratched the surface of the hard rocky shell we call the Earth's crust. Scientists freely admit their lack of knowledge about what lies deep within the 30 miles of continental crust that surrounds our world, since we've barely been able to drill a quarter of the way down. And that's only in easily accessible geographic areas.

Man-Made Underground Facilities

Can deep subterranean facilities be constructed? Yes indeed. Mankind has the technology to build such facilities, so it goes without saying that aliens do. I'm sure most of you have heard about the military facilities that we have built below the surface to withstand nuclear attacks. And man-made subterranean facilities are not rare. They're surprisingly plentiful, and include such things as railways, tunnels, metro systems, and power plants. Richard Sauder (1995) notes the power plant at Portage Mountain Dam in British Columbia that was built 400 ft below the surface. He also mentions plans being discussed by our Los Alamos National Laboratory, which itself was built underground, to build a physics test facility up to 6000 feet below the surface. Sauder lists a few man-made subterranean facilities as follows:

The Ritchie Facility

- The *Ritchie Facility*, also called *Raven Rock* and *Site R*, is a large, secure, underground military installation just on the southern Pennsylvania side of the Mason-Dixon line near the town of Blue Ridge Summit. It occupies 265,000 square feet, and lies 650 feet underground. It is composed of five buildings located in caverns artificially excavated for that purpose. Raven Rock is accessed via entrances dug out of the sides of the nearby mountainside. Site R is equipped with all the conveniences of a modern strip mall: stores, gyms, hair salons, restaurants, and all necessary utilities. Ritchie Facility is not normally listed in military installation guides; and for good reason. It is a very sensitive area that functions, in effect, like a back-up Pentagon, and can quickly assume the operations command-center with formidable supercomputing capabilities. It is said to be connected via long tunnels to the presidential retreat at Camp David, which is several miles away.

Please note the fact that this facility and its entrance points are located near a mountain, bearing in mind that mountains are one of the entrance points for underground UFO bases. We apparently have the same notion as our alien neighbors that such areas provide the best cover for secret underground installations. Or perhaps you think it's just a one-time coincidence that this subterranean facility is also near a mountain. Au contraire! Take a look at the next couple of facilities.

James Edward Gilmer

NORAD

Although the North American Aerospace Defense Command (NORAD) is a super secure facility, it isn't so secret anymore. Many people know it's situated deep within Cheyenne Mountain near Colorado Springs, Colorado. Many also know that NORAD uses its cutting-edge technology to monitor and collect information on everything related to air, space, and missile activity that may be useful to high-level government policy makers. Not as many people know, however, that the entrance tunnel through the mountain is 4,675 feet long, 22.5 feet high, and 25 feet wide, or that the central access tunnel that branches off from the entrance tunnel is 25 feet high and 45 feet wide. And this is all at surface level. No exact figures on depth are available, but it's much deeper than the Ritchie Facility's 650 foot depth. NORAD also has a similar secret underground command facility that it runs jointly with Canada near North Bay, Ontario.

FEMA

The Federal Emergency Management Agency (FEMA) operates other super secure underground government command installations. FEMA is well known for its leading role in coordinating emergency relief efforts following natural disasters, but not so well known for activities related to its sensitive role as a back-up government in national crises, such as nuclear war. One of these facilities is located inside of Mount Weather, near the northern Virginia town of Bluemont. According to Sauder, this is the "hub of the FEMA subterranean network," funded by "black money" and so secret that it's unlisted in FEMA publications. Deep below Mt. Weather, there is said to be an area resembling a small town in terms of its space, features, and facilities. It includes, a hospital, restaurant, streets, sidewalks, residential quarters, sewage operations, a communications system that includes tv and radio, and even a small lake! There are several other underground FEMA installations with supportive roles. Among them, one built below Mount Pony near Culpepper, Virginia; and others in Olney and Laytonsville, Maryland.

These few examples of man-made subterranean facilities merely scratch the surface of the total number that we have built. And I, for one, am certain that many of our underground facilities are even more secret than some of the ones mentioned above. Hopefully the ones that I listed are enough to illustrate my point that, since we are able to hollow out huge mountains and underground areas and to build small towns inside of them, unbeknownst to most of our own population, how many more bases could aliens have established at even deeper underground levels with their far more advanced technology?

Polar Access Areas?

In earlier sections of this book, we've examined sightings of UFOs near such underground *access* areas as mountains, forests, water and icy areas. Let's take another look at some of the icy areas, more specifically arctic regions.

Richard Byrd's Polar Flights

Rear Admiral Richard E. Byrd made official survey flights over the Arctic and Antarctic regions, and both times, according to Dr. Raymond Bernard (1979) and others, claimed to have seen astounding things. Most relevant to our discussion was that Byrd allegedly reported seeing UFOs flying near the poles. Another of Bernard's assertions, if true, is perhaps even more astounding: Byrd claimed to have flown into openings to the Earth's interior both times. In 1947, during his flight above the Arctic Circle near the North Pole, he and his crew were reportedly stunned to suddenly find themselves flying over 1700 miles of fresh water lakes, green vegetation, and grazing animals, rather than the frozen land that they had expected. Byrd also claimed that at least one of the creatures grazing on the green grass below resembled a wooly mammoth! During his flight, he and his crew radioed blow-by-blow descriptions of what was unfolding below, and immediately after returning from his flight, Byrd submitted a written report of what he and his crew had seen. Although the contents of the report were described as highly unusual, there were no official accusations that Byrd his crew were untruthful or suffered from mass hallucinations. On the contrary, Byrd was sent on another polar survey flight in 1956; this time the Antarctic Circle near the South Pole. Shockingly, Byrd saw many of the same things there as he saw up north over the Arctic Circle! And this time his flight over tropical land lasted for 2300 miles. Again, he made radio reports during the flight and a written report afterwards.

What Byrd and his crews actually flew over will always be debated. Some say that Dr. Bernard and others who reported Byrd's experiences were stretching the truth. Others say Byrd and his crews suffered mass hallucination. Still others, especially hollow-Earth believers, say that Byrd flew into a gradually sloping entrance into the Earth's hollow interior. Well, the Earth is definitely not hollow, but if researchers like Dr. Bernard are not dismissed as liars or quacks, one has to ask where the tropical flora and fauna seen by Byrd and his crews came from. If they really saw these things, a plausible answer is that they indeed flew into gradual entrances to some type of underground place. Not to a hollow interior, but possibly to a sub-surface area the was warm and spacious enough to foster tropical conditions and life forms. If so, perhaps animals that normally dwell at some subterranean level sometimes wander out. This would certainly explain why the carcasses of wooly mammoths sometimes found frozen in the ice are often so perfectly preserved and fresh that their flesh is still edible. It would also identify possible subterranean entrance points for UFOs. Recall that Byrd reported UFO sightings in these regions.

Underwater Entrances or Bases?

A very interesting and significant point about the UFO-water connection is that, according to many estimates, over half of all UFO sightings involve water. That is, UFOs are sighted either entering, exiting, or flying above water more than fifty percent of the time! And that doesn't even include thousands of UFOs seen in areas near water. This is an amazing statistic that immediately suggests to me a special UFO-water connection. One that probably includes underwater entrances to subterranean UFO bases. Bear in mind that if aliens can create underground entrances through the continental crust they can certainly do it through the oceanic crust. They would also have much more privacy and convenience creating such entrances underwater.

Some researchers maintain, however, that this UFO-water connection is more likely an indication of UFO bases established underwater. That is another distinct possibility that would also explain the high frequency of UFO sightings near water. As a matter of fact, I believe there is a strong likelihood that both exist. That is, aliens have both established underwater UFO bases and created underwater entrances to the Earth's interior. They would both certainly be convenient to have. Therefore, as you examine the following sections on sightings near water, keep an open mind. You could be reading about underwater bases, entrances, or both!

The Bermuda Triangle

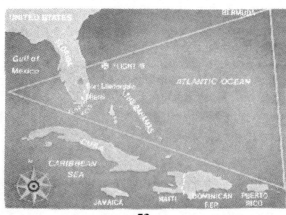

53

As you've undoubtedly read or heard, many air and sea craft have mysteriously vanished beneath the area of the Atlantic that forms a triangle with points near Bermuda, Puerto Rico and a few miles west of southern Florida in the Gulf of Mexico (figure 53). Figure 54 is an example of the numerous

Chariots of Gods or Demons?
The Incredible Truth About UFOs and Extraterrestrials

JANUARY 31 1948

31 MISSING IN AIR LINER

NOW "PRESUMED LOST"

ALL-DAY SEARCH OFF BERMUDA

The British South American Airways Tudor IV aircraft Star Tiger, reported missing yesterday, with 25 passengers and a crew of six on board, on its way to Bermuda, is now presumed lost, according to a Ministry of Civil Aviation statement issued last night.

54

press articles on inexplicable disappearances in this area. It is called the Bermuda Triangle and the Devil's Triangle, and has been known for centuries as a place where strange sightings, ships and aircraft disappearances, and other unusual phenomena occur.

Public focus on the Bermuda Triangle was suddenly magnified with the disappearance of Flight 19 on December 5, 1945. Flight 19, comprising five torpedo bombers, had taken off from Fort Lauderdale on a training mission through the triangle (see figure 55). About two hours after take-off, Flight 19 began having instrument problems. Flight leader Lieutenant Charles Taylor radioed in that he was disoriented: "Both my compasses are out...I'm over land, but it's broken. I'm sure I'm in the Keys, but I don't know how far down and I don't know how to get to Fort Lauderdale."

Over the next two hours Taylor made several fragmented radio calls, after which, the flight just vanished without a trace, presumable somewhere beneath the waves. A five-day search involving dozen and air and sea craft failed to turn up any clue as to the flight's whereabouts; not even an oil slick where it might have gone down. This was just one of the many such incidents that **(Flight 19 before its disappearance)** have been reported since then. (Reader's Digest)

The Bermuda Triangle disappearances have at least some of the earmarks of a UFO presence. First of all, as in the case of flight 19, cockpit electronic instrumentation and ship or

55

plane compasses go haywire. An interruption in power may also happen. In Chapter four (Gut Alt Gossen sighting) we discussed how this disruptive effect can cause engines to stall. Second, this happened over water, which again, most likely serves as the main UFO portal from the surface to underground bases and vice-versa. In summary, Bermuda Triangle disappearances are likely a result of the fact that this area contains several entrance points to subterranean and submarine UFO bases.

Japan's Devil's Triangle

There are also other large bodies of water where ships and aircraft experience electrical disturbances and inexplicably disappear. One is the area of the Pacific ocean between Japan and the Marianas Islands, referred to by some as the *Japanese Devil's Triangle*. For centuries villagers in that area have passed on stories of demons who lurk beneath the ocean and destroy ships that sail on the waves above. Modern attention on this area intensified in September 1952 when the Japanese research ship Fifth Kaiyo-Maru suddenly vanished without a trace. Nearly as disturbing as the disappearance itself was the fact that radio contact with the ship had been abruptly lost before it vanished, which further hindered rescue efforts. Since then, there have been dozens of such disappearances under similar circumstances in the region. Again, as with Flight 19 in the Bermuda Triangle, there was evidence of some type of field that disrupted electrical equipment, which, in the Maru's case, involved the radio. This is therefore another possible location for multiple entrances to underground and/or underwater UFO bases. (Story)

There is a remarkable fact about Japan's Devil's Triangle and the Bermuda Triangle that you should note. If you draw a line straight down from one, you will eventually encounter the other.

The Great Lakes Triangle

Like the Bermuda Triangle and Japan's Devil's Triangle, the waters of the Great Lakes are steeped in centuries-old lore of inexplicable disasters and disappearances. The Great Lakes comprise Lake Erie, Lake Huron, Lake Ontario, Lake Michigan, and Lake Superior. Boasting about 100,000 square miles, they form the largest single area of fresh water in the world, which increases the likelihood of UFO activity there. An incident that typifies aircraft disappearances in that area ocurred over Lake Erie in 1966 when a pilot on a routine flight suddenly radioed a distress call to Cleveland Air Traffic Control Center. His cockpit instrumentation had stopped functioning and as a result, he had no sense of orientation. His final message to the control center was that his plane was spiraling downward out of control.

Lake Ontario is said to be one of the more active Lakes in terms of UFO sightings. The types of UFOs seen most frequently here are orange-colored spheres that zoom around at unbelievable speeds. When they aren't flying in the sky above, they often land on the water or dive down into the water.

An interesting sighting occurred over Lake Michigan in 1978. On the morning of July 23, personnel from area Coast Guard stations reported spotting a cigar-shaped object flying over the lake. Witnesses reported getting a clear look at the object and described it as silver in color with flashing lights of various colors around it. It stopped in mid-air and hovered for about 30 minutes at an altitude of about 2000 yards. Suddenly it took off at a blinding rate of speed and vanished from sight. (Story)

The tell-tale signs of a UFO presence are unmistakable. The trouble with his instruments and his stalled engine are the most obvious signs. "Strange lights" are among the phenomena seen in this area, both below the waves and in the sky above them. Such sightings coupled with incidents like the ones over Lake Erie and Lake Ontario make it even more apparent that UFOs maintain a constant presence in the Great Lakes; a presence which most likely include entrances to subterranean bases. As further confirmation of the UFO-water connection, let's examine a few more water-related sightings in the next section.

More UFOs Sightings Over Water

On November 12, 1887, near Cape Race, Newfoundland, a large luminous spherical object was spotted flying out of the water near the British ship *Siberian*. Captain Moore reported that it hovered about 50 feet in the air, then moved slowly toward the ship where it hovered for a while longer before flying away.

Another incident occurred over the Atlantic Ocean on August 4, 1950. According to the research of Lawrence Fawcett and Barry Greenwood, the captain of a ship traveling from Nova Scotia to an East Coast U.S. port was alerted by members of his crew to the presence of an unidentified object flying about 100 feet overhead. The captain got a clear view of it through his binoculars and described it as cylindrical in shape, silvery in color, and completely silent as it paced the ship at a position directly above the starboard bow. The object then sped up and passed the ship at a tremendous rate of speed and disappeared.

Ivan Sanderson reported an incident that took place in 1945 involving the sighting of a unidentified object coming from underwater. A U.S. military ship, the *Delarof*, was transporting munitions in the Northeast Pacific when crew members spotted a huge spherical object flying out of the ocean. The object, estimated at about 200 feet in diameter and completely noiseless, hovered for a while above the Delarof, circled it a few times, then hovered motionlessly again.

After another few minutes it suddenly bolted out of view with tremendous acceleration.

Again, most UFO sightings are water related, so, as you can imagine, these are but a minuscule number of the documented reports. An interesting common denominator among these UFOs is that they all hovered for a while in a manner that apparently indicated that they were *observing* the human gawkers below them. Sound familiar? At any rate, I'm sure you now agree that, given the evidence that we've discussed on the UFO-water connection, underwater bases and portals to subterranean UFO bases are, at the very least, a strong likelihood. Let's now consider the concept of underground UFO bases from another angle; namely strong indications that our ancestors were aware of them. That's right, our ancestors knew that aliens had subterranean bases! You'll see proof of this in the next section.

Myths Are Based on Reality

Your first question is undoubtedly why this section is about myths when I promised you proof that our ancestors knew of underground alien bases. Well, this section is actually on both. My initial aim is to show you that our forefathers' awareness of subterranean bases is reflected in the myths that they passed on to us. First of all, let's make sure we're on the same page regarding the definition of myth. This word has a number of usages and connotations, but nowadays refers almost exclusively to an idea or story from a particular culture that is meant to convey some historical or cosmological truth but that is unfounded and therefore considered imaginary. In my view, although some myths have foundations that have not yet been verified, they all have some degree of reality at their cores. The degree of reality is, of course, more apparent in some myths than in others. Let's look at some of the more apparent ones.

The City of Ur

The Biblical city of Ur is a prime example of a reality-based myth. Most people used to scoff at the notion that it was once a city in ancient Mesopotamia, even though the Bible clearly states that the Old Testament patriarch Abraham had come from there. Even now many people doubt the historical accuracy of the Bible, considering it instead largely a collection of fictional literature, symbolic stories and verses pieced together to impart certain religious messages. In other words, a collection of imaginative myths. But the fact is, many of these stories are turning out to have solid kernels of truth in them, and it's no different with Ur. You see, Ur, a center of Sumerian civilization about 5000 years ago, was discovered during excavations by Leonard Wooley, and its existence is now an historical fact.

The Iliad and the Odyssey

Greek mythology is another source of reality. The people, places, and events in Homer's *Iliad* and *Odyssey*, for example. Little more than a century ago, scholars thought it ludicrous to consider Troy anything more than a product of Homer's imagination. Well, as Andrew Tomas aptly describes, in 1870, Heinrich Schliemann discovered Troy exactly where it was in the Iliad! Afterwards, he traced the route of Odysseus's voyage homeward and, remembering Homer's description in the Iliad of Odysseus's cup, he found it in a deep shaft!

The Flood

One of the most well-known of myths shared by various cultures is that of a widespread flood.

Most of us are familiar with the Old Testament account of global inundation, but not many know that the Biblical version was preceded by one in the epic of *Gilgamesh*, a poem originating in Mesopotamia around 5000 years ago in the Akkadian language. This Sumerian classic was once thought to be purely fictional mythology. Now, however, we know that Gilgamesh really did exist as the king of Uruk in about the 3rd millennium BC. What's more, those of you who have read this epic, know that its description of a catastrophic flood is amazingly similar to that of the Old Testament. In South America, the Sun God of Andean culture sent a cataclysmic flood to afflict the world. The Quiche Mayan *Popol-Vuh* (Book of Advice) mentions the gods being dissatisfied with the people they had created and sending a great flood to wipe them out. Indian myths include a devastating deluge along with a forewarning to the first man, Manu, who proceeds to build an ark for safety. In China, the Thunder God caused a global deluge. Greek mythology has a version of a great flood sent by Zeus as punishment for Prometheus's offenses. So, as you can see, the myth of diluvial devastation is shared by most ancient cultures. And ongoing research and exploration are providing more and more confirmation that such a flood did indeed wash over extensive areas of the world.

James Edward Gilmer

Atlantis?

An ancient myth whose reality core is steadily gaining in credence is that of the continent of Atlantis. Its most well-known believer was none other than Greek philosopher Plato (figure 56), who described it with surprising detail in his *Timaeus and Critias*. He stated that it had existed nearly 12,000 years ago just beyond the Pillars of Hercules (Gibraltar) in the Atlantic Ocean (named after the mythical continent). He also said it was a wealthy and powerful empire whose harbors were always filled with ships from the many lands that it traded with. Finally, Plato related that Atlantis had met its demise from sudden devastating earthquakes and floods causing it to sink literally overnight.

56

Although some theories on the location of Atlantis place it in various spots around the world, the Atlantic is by far the area mentioned most. Furthermore, virtually all who believe it existed in the Atlantic pinpoint its exact location as inside the Bermuda Triangle. Some post-Plato believers describe it as being technologically advanced and using flying machines as one of its modes of travel. They also believe that Atlantis was more likely destroyed by nuclear warfare than a natural catastrophe. Still others say that Atlanteans had highly developed psychic abilities and used crystals to amplify and direct these powers, and that the misuse of such powers caused their destruction. By their account, such misuse led to the sudden uncontrollable discharge of tremendously destructive energy from one or more of their giant crystals, and thereby to their demise.

Whichever description of Atlantis turns out to be the most accurate, the fact remains that a growing body of evidence strongly suggests that Atlantis was a real continent that sank in the Atlantic Ocean. According to Charles Berlitz, the history of many countries included stories of an island or civilization that disappeared into the Atlantic Ocean before the Biblical flood. Among them, the Guanche (Canary Islands) spoke of *Atalaya*, which was an empire in the Atlantic that sank. The Basques said it was *Atalaintika*. To Aztecs, it was *Aztlan*, their original home. The Mayans called it both *Aztlan* and *Atlan*. Other native tribes in the Americas also called it Atlan. The Toltecs referred to it as *Tlapallan*. Is it just a coincidence that all these names sound so similar, or are they all describing the same place?

Another fact that supports the existence of Atlantis is that the parts of the Bermuda Triangle where Atlantis was said to have sunk are now known to have existed above water for thousands of years before sinking. A case in point involves, the presence of stalagmites and stalagtites within a vast system of underwater caves called the *Blue Holes*, as Berlitz so aptly describes, these icicle-like rock formations shape themselves by drippings from cave ceilings when the caves are above water, meaning that they must have formed before the caves sank beneath the waves. Furthermore, although coral formations normally develop near the surface, many have been found very deep underwater. Other indications of a sunken continent are deep beaches and samples of igneous granite, which are virtually incontrovertible evidence that a continent sank there.

The most impressive evidence in support of Atlantis may be the ruins found off the coasts of the Bahamian islands of Bimini and Andros. These ruins are believed by many to be the remains of man-made structures that sank thousands of years ago. They include portions of buildings and walls on the bottom of the ocean. The clearest and most convincing of these ruins is a system of large, mostly rectangular stones called the *Bimini Road* or the *Bimini Wall* (see drawing in figure 57). The huge flat stones lie almost flush against each other in a consistent, artificial-looking pattern about 2000 feet long, and form what looks like either a road or a long wall that fell over with the stones still in place. Many expert geologists say the stones are too neatly and strategically placed to be a natural formation. One more item of note that may not be significant to some and very important to others: The Bimini Road was discovered in 1968—the year predicted by the great clairvoyant Edgar Cayce as the year in which parts of Atlantis would be rediscovered!

57

James Edward Gilmer

Sumerian Myths

About 6000 years ago, the Sumerians passed on a myth based on the notion that our solar system consisted of a sun orbited by planets. This certainly predated the theory of Copernicus by quite a few centuries. Another equally amazing part of the myth is its assertion that our solar system contains 10 planets. Bear in mind that before the 18th century only six planets were recognized by scholars. Uranus, Neptune, and Pluto weren't discovered until 1781, 1846, and 1930 respectively. But what about the fact that we only officially recognize nine planets not ten? That's certainly true, but many scientists are beginning to re-examine that assumption and are allowing the possibility of a tenth planet. Back in 1978 a celestial body was discovered very close to Pluto. It's called Charon and it orbits Pluto. Most of the astronomical community refer to it as a moon, because it's smaller than and orbits Pluto. Some, however, refer to it as a planet, because it is so close in size to Pluto. Before Charon was discovered, Earth's moon, with a diameter one quarter that of Earth was considered disproportionately large compared to the size of other moons in proportion to their orbital planets. But Charon is over half the size of Pluto! Is Charon the tenth planet of the Sumerian myth? Where did the Sumerians get their information?

African Dogon Myths

Perhaps the most astounding of all myths proven to have a core of reality involves a key part of the cosmology of a small African tribe called the *Dogon*, who now live in Mali. This millennia-old myth begins with the Dogon belief that their people originated in a double star system. One that includes two stars—Sirius, aka Alpha Canis Majoris or the Dog Star, and a smaller companion star known as the Digitaria star. The first astonishing fact that immediately becomes clear is that a simple tribe of people, with no

58

astronomical instruments or calculation systems could know that Sirius was part of a double star system. After all, although Sirius (Sirius A) (See brightest object in figure 58) is the brightest star in our night skies, the smaller star, Sirius B is not visible to the naked eye. As a matter of fact, it wasn't even visible to telescopes until the late 19th century, and not officially verified until 1970! It had been simply too small and undetectable in the glare of the much brighter Sirius A. Thus the Dogon possess ancient astronomical knowledge that was just recently discovered by modern scientists. But how?

And that's not all. According to some very interesting research done by Robert Temple, other even more amazing parts of this Dogon myth presuppose a knowledge of astrophysics and even nuclear physics that rivals our highest current scientific knowledge in these areas. Consider the following partial list:

- The Dogon myth teaches that Sirius B is smaller but heavier than Sirius A. This is absolutely right. One would naturally assume that the larger star would be the heavier, which normally occurs with *main sequence* stars. But what makes this Dogon myth so shocking in its correctness, is that we now know that Sirius B is not a main sequence star, but rather a *white dwarf*. This is the hot core that remains of a low-mass star, which, in its death throes has swollen to a red giant and then blown off its outer layers as planetary nebula. This core is now no more than 50% larger than the Earth in diameter, but is so dense that it contains nearly as much mass as our sun. Thus, only someone with a background in nuclear physics could have known that Sirius B is heavier than Sirius A. So how could the ancient Dogon have known?

- The Dogon myth states that Sirius B orbits Sirius A every 50 years. Exactly right. We've only very recently verified this.

- The Dogon myth indicates that Sirius B orbits Sirius A in an elliptical fashion. Verified. As a matter of fact, most orbits are elliptical to some extent, but again, astronomical instruments and calculations are needed to determine this.

- The Dogon myth notes that Sirius B rotates on its own axis. Correct. Most celestial bodies do the same thing, but this fact presupposes a modern knowledge of astronomy.

The most obvious question is how the Dogon came upon knowledge of the Sirius star system that we didn't even know until recently. They didn't have the scientific know-how to collect this information, so only two other logical possibilities come to mind. One, they were given this information by someone. But since no one on this Earth had such knowledge to give, it would have had to come from someone not of this Earth, right? Two, their ancestors really did originate from the Sirius system. Actually, there is truth in both of these suggestions, which we'll examine again a little later.

At this point, let's make a quick mental note of what we've just discussed; namely, the fact that, although myths are generally regarded as fictitious, they are all based on reality. And although their external forms may distort the facts somewhat, they still reflect something that actually occurred or existed. We've illustrated this by pointing out several myths that have been proven to contain a core of truth. My next proposition is that, if we accept the general premise that myths are based on reality, we should be consistent. That is, if we acknowledge the concept that myths have a truthful core, we should not arbitrarily exclude any from acceptance, regardless of how incredible they might sound. After all, how credible could the Dogon myth have sounded to scientists just a couple hundred years ago? Okay, now assuming the existence of some degree of truth in all myths, let's apply this assumption to some myths related to the general topic of this chapter. Let's now examine some myths that may describe alien inhabitants of the Earth's interior!

Myths About Underground Races

Eskimos

The myths of several different cultures tell of people who live underground and of surface openings that lead down to their homes. The North Pole, for example is said, to be an access point to the underworld (recall Richard Byrd's experiences there). As Raymond Bernard notes, the Eskimos are one of these cultures. Their myths, like those of many others, say that the Earth's interior is inhabited by a race of people with brown skin and small bodies (recall one of the descriptions of aliens in the first chapter). They also claim that the Eskimos themselves are descendants of underworld people. Other cultural myths also describe the Eskimos in this manner. For instance, a Norwegian myth says that Eskimos originated from supernatural beings inside of the Earth.

Native Americans

The native cultures of North and South America also pass on myths about subterranean ancestry. The Incas, for example, believe that their ancestors originally came from the interior to the surface of the earth through caves and openings in Lake Titicaca. Navajo progenitors are also said to have ascended to the surface from below through openings. Pueblo Indians traditionally make a small hole in the floor of their ceremonial chambers to symbolize their myth regarding the Arctic opening that leads to the underworld home of their ancestors. The myths of several Indian tribes, including the Apaches, speak of large underground tunnels which were excavated by energy beams used by beings from outer space!

The Nagas of India

Ancient Sanskrit texts contain several references to extraterrestrial beings who visited the Earth. One of these involves the *Nagas*, or Serpent Gods who flew to Earth and then set up their dwellings underground near the Himalayas. The Nagas were said to make long and frequent flights through the skies before returning to their subterranean dwellings. According to Andrew Tomas, the Nagas are so ingrained in the Indian psyche that they are to modern-day Indian motion pictures what Martians are to Americans.

Agharta

Asian myths include a legendary subterranean world with the Buddhist name Agharta, whose capital is the equally legendary city of Shambhala. As Peter Kolosimo points out, Hindu and Buddhist myths say that Agartha was established somewhere beneath the Himalayas about 600,000 years ago. It is inhabited by beings with special abilities who originated in outer space and arrived in space ships! In addition, these beings periodically come to the surface world to check on the progress of mankind. A couple of noteworthy observations: First, Agartha is said to to be under a mountain range. Mountains, if you recall, are one of the frequent geographical haunts of UFOs and, again, one of the likely areas for subterranean openings. Second, beings from outer space that periodically check on humans? Sound vaguely familiar? Is it just coincidental that the second point is consistent with the aliens' mission on Earth?

Norse Myths

According to Norse mythology, there were two races of Gods, the Aesir, who were sky gods, and the Vanir who were earth gods. Mythologist Roy Willis notes that both races have dwellings in the heavens, which is presumably Asgard, and that the Vanir also have a subterranean dwelling called Vanaheim. In addition, the Vanir had a magical ship that could travel anywhere, in the sky or under the earth.

Let's step back and review some of the elements of these myths within the context of this book, bearing in mind that these represent just a fraction of the total number of similar myths that exist. First of all, myths about underground beings are virtually everywhere in the world, which enhances the likelihood that they're based on reality. Second, most of the beings involved possess some special quality that distinguishes them from *regular* people. Next, in a number of cases, these special beings use ships that can fly. And finally, direct reference is sometimes made to the extraterrestrial origin of the beings. Are all these just coincidences? Should we be inconsistent and dismiss these myths as too fanciful? In the next section we will review some claims of actual sightings of UFO bases.

Nazi German Belief in an Underworld

So you thought that belief in an underworld was limited to ancient and primitive cultures? What about the government of the most technologically advanced culture in the world in the 1940s? That's right. Although one of the most ruthless regimes in history, Nazi Germany had the world's most brilliant scientists and wielded the world's most ingenious weapons, and yet believed that an advanced race of

humanoid beings lived in the interior of the Earth! They were also convinced that these beings came to the surface at times to mingle with humans. As Brad Steiger (1973) explains, in April 1942, while the Nazi war machine was fully engaged on the battlefield, Nazi scientists were embarking on a search for an entrance to the underworld–with the blessings and support of the German government, including the Fuehrer Adolf Hitler, SS and Gestapo chief Heinrich Himmler, and Hitler's deputy Hermann Goering. Their plan, after finding the subterranean entrance, was to convince the advanced beings to genetically mix with Germans to form a new master race! It goes without saying that they never found the entrance, but I think my point has been made: A culture as technologically sophisticated as Nazi Germany must have had some pretty convincing evidence to lead it to search for an underground race of alien beings.

Locations of Underground UFO Bases?

Getting a detailed report on a UFO sighting is often difficult enough. Getting a report of any kind on an underground alien base is understandably much more so. Fortunately, I managed to find several such reports, some more detailed than others. The ones listed below are from a book with very limited circulation entitled *Underground Alien Bases*. The author is a retired military officer who opted to remain anonymous. Although I have not seen any corroboration of this information, I give it at least some credence, because the areas mentioned are known to be high-activity areas for UFOs. The following are four of the more interesting ones.

Mount Rainier, Washington?

The existence of an alien base below Mount Rainier region shouldn't be that much of a surprise. After all, as I'm sure you recall, this area contains mountains and is where Kenneth Arnold made his famous *saucer* sighting. It is also a region rich in ancient Indian myths about beings who could fly. UFOs of various shapes and sizes here are still being reported. A group of researchers climbed the easternmost of the two craters there and discovered a huge aperture about 1000 feet wide and 500 feet deep that descended gradually downward. After following the sloping pathway for a while, they discovered a huge system of tunnels and enormous halls. They also encountered strange, unsettling noises coming from places deep with the tunnels. After continuing with no apparent end in sight, the group halted its trek and returned to the surface.

Mount Lassen, California?

Another mountainous region with an opening to an underground base. Lassen National Forest, another possible entry point, is in the vicinity. Actually, this area under Tehama County is reported to be one of the underground cities that I mentioned at the beginning of this chapter. The main type of craft seen here is said to be mainly saucer or disk shaped, but "orange fireballs" are also seen entering and exiting the area.

Mount Shasta, California?

This underground base is loaded with possible entrance points. First there is Mount Shasta itself. Then, Mount Shasta is literally surrounded by forest areas: Shasta National Forest, Klamath National Forest, and Salmon-Trinity Alps Wilderness, which, of course, are also high activity area for UFOs. There is said to be a vast tunnel and cavern network on the way to the base below.

James Edward Gilmer

Brown Mountain, North Carolina?

This base is situated below Brown Mountain in the general area of Morgantown, North Carolina. Mysterious lights have reportedly been seen for centuries darting around the sky above Brown Mountain and in the valley below it. According to one account, a researcher embarked on a private expedition to Brown Mountain to verify or disprove the rumored UFO sightings in the area. Camping out there one evening, he spotted a bright circular object rising out of a large opening in the ground. Soon other similar objects followed it out until there were 20 or more flying around!

Chapter 8

Aliens: Their Origin And Links to Mankind

Gods or Pilots?

Let's put into proper perspective the divinity attributed to many of the beings that ancient people called *gods*. If you will, try to imagine yourself living in the same time and place as some of the ancient peoples and their pantheons. Let's say you lived 3,000 years ago on a Pacific island. Everything in your life is primitive; your living conditions, your attitudes, your comprehension of physical principles and concepts. One day, as your tribe is out hunting or gathering fruits and berries for its next meal, some strange objects swoop down out of the sky like giant birds and land in front of you. Then, while you're frozen with fear and awe, some beings come out of the flying vessels and walk toward you. They resemble humans, but they have unusually pale skin and they're wearing garments that no one had ever seen before. They proceed show you wondrous devices like enchanted cylinders that emit rays of light (flashlights), magic boxes that spew flickering flames (cigarette lighters) and divine potions that made them feel better (medicine). What would you do? What would you think?

Now honestly, if you had experienced this scenario you would have probably bowed down and worshiped those beings as gods, right? Sure you would've. Do you know how I know? Because this scenario that I just painted for you was not an imaginary one from three thousand years ago. It actually happened just a few decades ago during WWII! No kidding! As Berlitz (1973) points out, native villagers of New Guinea referred to World War II pilots as "white gods" who brought all kinds of remarkable things and magic medicines to them. And for decades after the war, the natives continued to draw pictures and carve wooden images of these divine beings and their ships and jeeps with the hope that they would one day return from the skies!

Gods From Other Planets?

If the situation described above in New Guinea could happen in the 20th century, is it really a stretch of the imagination to say that it happened to most cultures that existed millenia ago? Isn't it more likely that myths of gods coming from the skies were the authors' primitive descriptions of extraterrestrial beings? Recalling the core reality of myths, many cultures teach of ancestors and creators who come from other planets and star systems, and who are often viewed as divine beings. The origin myth of the African Dogon (as you recall, they correctly described the Sirius double star system) included beings called *Nommos*, who are regarded as the "founders" of Dogon civilization. These Nommos came to the Earth from the Sirius system in flying vessels that whirled and made loud noises. According to mythologist Willis, other African tribes—the Fipas of Tanzania and the Tutsis of Rwanda—believe that their ancestors were semi-divine beings who came from the sky.

The people of Sumer believed that the *Anunnaki* came to Earth from another planet in our solar system called Nebiru. Like the Dogon, the Sumerian myth demonstrated astronomical knowledge that current science has just recently caught up with. For instance, the Sumerian model of our solar system included several planets revolving around a sun–and this was over 5000 years ago! Actually this model indicated twelve planets, so maybe we haven't quite caught up with it yet. At any rate, if these gods were not extraterrestrial pilots, then who gave the Sumerians and Dogon their unusual knowledge?

Many other myths apparently showed more interest in the stellar origin of alien visitors than in their possible divinity. Kolosimo (1973) notes that the Haida Indians of the Queen Charlotte Islands in Canada speak of "great sages descended from the stars on discs of fire." The Navajos speak of "creatures who came from the sky and stayed a long time on Earth but finally returned to their world." These aliens were said to have taken several willing Ojibway tribesmen back to their planet with them. Among Oceanic people, the Maoris await the promised return of the "great wizards from the skies" who remained on Earth for awhile and then "flew away on their colored ships."

The ancient Indian epic, the *Mahabharata*, speaks often of a flying machine called the *Vimana*. The son of the wind, Bhima was said to fly with his Vimana which was made of metal, had wings, emitted a trail and made a loud noise. Sounds like a modern plane, doesn't it? Another great Indian epic, the *Ramayana*, describes another type of Vimana, saying that they were circular craft with portholes and a dome, and that they were flown at great heights with the aid of fuel that resembled quicksilver and a propulsive wind. They could travel at tremendous speeds, hover motionlessly or maneuver in all directions. Are you thinking what I'm thinking? Yes, they were flying saucers!

Scientific Proof That Gods Were Aliens?

The Chinese have an interesting myth about beings that descended from the heavens about 12,000 years ago. Kolosimo (1973) describes them as humanoids with yellowish skin, huge heads, and short thin bodies, who landed on Earth in ships and tried to establish contact with the local cave-dwellers. This story has an ironic twist, though. Instead of bowing in abject humility and worshiping these strange visitors as gods, the Chinese natives rejected and even attacked them, because they were so repulsively ugly!

Sounds too fantastic to be true even for a book about UFOs, right? Well, consider this: Buried in tombs inside those same caves, archaeologists recently discovered skeletons that were found to be about 12,000 years old. Furthermore, upon closer inspection, the skeletons were those of humanoids with short thin frames and disproportionately large skulls! To top it all off, ancient paintings on the cave walls depicted what appeared to be a fleet of space ships flying away from the sun, moon, and stars, towards a mountainous area of the Earth! Just an unusual string of coincidences?

Gods or Demons?

In the above section, the ancient Chinese apparently thought that their alien visitors were too ugly to be gods. This was an exceptional case, of course. In most cases, primitive Earthlings worshiped alien beings, although not always as good gods. Sometimes they considered them evil or demonic. The Maya, for instance, had good gods from the skies, and evils ones from the underworld. Even today, most people associate the sky with something positive, like Heaven, and the underground with something negative, like Hell. Mayans were no different. It's noteworthy that the greatest of their good gods from the skies, Itzamna, was said to have lizard-like qualities. As you recall, lizard features are not uncommon among reported descriptions of aliens. It's equally noteworthy that the most prominent of the evil underground gods was connected with a Jaguar because of the resemblance of the Jaguar's spotted hide to the starry sky. Now why would an underworld god be linked to the starry sky when there were already a number of recognized sky gods? Could it be that both sets of deities were known to come from above, but that one of them had chosen to establish a base in the Earth's interior while the others maintained bases on the Moon or Mars?

Why Did Aliens Come to Earth Originally?

Now that we have established the strong likelihood that aliens have had underground bases on Mars, the Moon and Earth for thousands of years, it's time to address the question of why they came. As I considered the possibilities, two stood out as the most plausible–catastrophe and exploration. Their home planet could have suffered some catastrophic mishap that rendered it uninhabitable. Such a calamity could result from a collision with a giant meteor or asteroid, a nuclear holocaust, a runaway greenhouse environment (like that on Venus), the scorching heat from a dying sun going supernova, as well as other possibilities. By the way, all stars, including our own Sun, will die sooner or later, usually in a violent manner. When that happens, the Earth, or what's left of it will become uninhabitable (if it isn't beforehand). So what does a race of technologically advanced beings do if something like this happens? What will we do when it happens to us in another few billion years? Do we stay and die with our planet? Of course not. By then, we'll have the technology for manned interstellar travel, and we'll most likely locate another habitable planet and settle there, right? And settling or colonizing might well have been what our extraterrestrial neighbors originally had in mind when they flew here.

Exploration is the other possible reason for their arrival. Exploration seems to be a natural inclination of all intelligent creatures and, of course, is the main motivation behind our own space missions. At our present level of technology, our manned exploration missions are limited to the Moon and could involve little more than the examination of soil and mineral samples. But civilizations with the advanced technology that extraterrestrials apparently have would include much more in their explorations. Their research would be much more comprehensive than ours, because they don't have the obvious limitations that we do. Their spaceships seem to have the capability go literally anywhere on Earth, including under ground and under water. In addition, their high-tech devices most likely allow them to collect and study much more than just a few scoops of surface soil.

Alien Genetic Intervention?

Current theories hold that *homo sapiens*, modern man, is somewhere between 200,000 and 2 million years old, with most being closer to the former than the latter. All, however, acknowledge that we made the transition from primitive hominid species in a surprisingly short time, "almost overnight." Researchers continue to search for the missing link that will explain how it happened so quickly. Among ufologists who know that the advent of UFOs on Earth predates that of modern man, however, the missing link is obvious: Extraterrestrials intervened in the genetic development of mankind! They did it in one of two ways, or possibly both. First, laboratory manipulation of our genetic codes. Second, hybridization; that is, genetic mixing of humans and extraterrestrials. Various myths indicate that aliens likely did both. This certainly provides justification for possible alien abductions. Wouldn't it be a logical step for scientists to periodically check on the results of their experiments?

Most myths that tell of man's creation involve forming man out of some type of natural material, mainly soil. The imagery of using materials from the earth is likely they only way the authors could convey the idea that aliens were working with the basic materials of life. The concepts of genes and chromosomes was certainly not within their comprehension. The notion of shaping these basic materials into humanoid form sounds very much like the authors' symbolic way of saying that the aliens manipulated these genes and chromosome in a certain way in order to produce modern man.

The Choco, Chibcha, and Hopi tribes of Latin America, for example, teach that the gods created man out of clay. One Greek myth indicates that man was created from *clay* and woman from *earth*. A clear reflection of the fact that different genetic and chromosomal (x and y) qualities were involved. The Incas say that the Creator, Viracocha not only created man out of clay, but also gave him various human behavioral characteristics. The Maya teach that their ancestors were created from a special blend of maize in order to give them divine understanding (greater intelligence?) and a strong reproductive drive. These last two examples clearly refer to genetic manipulation.

The Bagobo of the Philippine island of Mindanao have a myth that makes an even stronger reference to genetic manipulation. They teach that monkeys and humans once looked and behaved alike until the god Pamalak Bagobo created humans as a separate race. According to Chinese mythology, the goddess Nu Gua came to Earth from Heaven and shaped humans out of mud in her own image. An example of humans being genetically endowed with alien characteristics? The Yoruba of West Africa say that the gods created humans in the sky and then sent them down to earth. Does this indicate that the aliens' laboratories were in orbiting or hovering spaceships? Or maybe on Mars or the Moon?

Many myths indicate that aliens genetically altered humans through hybridization, which would entail test tube mixture of human and alien genes and/or actual copulation. The latter method was apparently common ancient times. To those who read the Old Testament, the most familiar example of such an ancient belief may be Genesis 6:1-2, which says: "And it came to pass, when men began to multiply on the face of the earth, and daughters were born unto them. That the sons of God saw the daughters of men that they were fair; and they took them wives of all which they chose." The first verse indicates that the human race is not that old. The second says that beings considered of divine origin, in Hebrew, the *Nephilim* or fallen ones, decided to mate with humans, thus adding a new element to the human gene pool. By the way, many Bible scholars interpret these fallen ones as the fallen angels who led to the presence of evil on Earth. In any case, there is unanimous agreement that the Nephilim were non-earthly beings. The author, unaware of the aliens' true agenda, naturally imputed human motivations for this mating; namely that the women were attractive.

There are other instances of hybrid offspring resulting from the sexual union between aliens and humans. Among oceanic cultures, the Maoris say that their civilization has its roots in a sexual liaison ages ago between sky people and a woman in their original tribe. There are even myths indicating that these types of relations were not always voluntary on the part of the humans. Among North

James Edward Gilmer

American Indians, the Quinalt teach that sky people who came from the stars abducted women apparently for the purpose of mating. According to the Yanomami of Venezuela, the god Omam engaged in more than one type of manipulation. First, they say that that human female genitalia were not suitable for mating with him, so he fashioned more suitable ones. This description may have been the Yanomani interpretation of some device that aided the sexual union with the woman. At any rate, the subsequent intercourse with her produced the Yanomami's ancestors. As far as Greek mythology goes, even the most casual of readers are likely aware that copulation between Earthlings and the Gods of Olympus was fairly commonplace.

The African Connection

Were Africans the First "Chosen People"?

The most widely held theory on the origin of mankind is the so-called "out of Africa" theory. It asserts that the first humans lived and developed into modern man there, and then migrated to other regions of the world. Recent genetic findings apparently bolster this view. These findings are based to a large extent on the examination of genes found in mitochondria. A mitochondrion is a round or oblong energy-producing structure in a cell that contains a different type of DNA (deoxyribonucleic acid) from that found in the chromosomes of cellular nuclei. While chromosomal genes are inherited from both parents, mitochondrial genes are inherited only from the mother and provide a reliable genetic path for tracing ancestry. The genetic tree diagrams generated in such research invariably suggest that the common ancestor of modern man was native to Africa.

60

Research has led to the discovery that, contrary to previous assumptions, no real differences exist between the so-called races of man. This realization has now negated *race* as a valid scientific term, at least in terms of popular assumptions underlying its use. Although racial categories may be still useful for purposes of ethnic identification, the external differences involved are due to the gene combinations that form rather than to actual differences in genes. In addition, there are more genetic variations among Africans than among non-

African groups, due to the fact that, as the most ancient group on Earth, Africans have had more time to develop such variations than have other groups.

So why the quick update on our genetic ancestry? Well, generally, to point out the fact that these findings have enabled a better contextual understanding of genetic intervention. More specifically, it has allowed us to identify Africans as the first group of humans that experienced alien intervention, meaning that subsequent intervention in non-African cultures occurred later, following the migration of their progenitors from Africa. This awareness might prove a useful research tool, particularly with regard to ascertaining time frames for intervention in specific cultures. It might also provide a possible clue as to why the astounding astrophysical information on the alien homeland in the Sirius star system was apparently given exclusively to the ancestors of the African Dogon (see Chapter 7).

Testimony by The Sphinx?

We've discussed the fact that myths always contain some degree of truth in their cores, and we've seen them in written and painted form. But what about sculptures? They can tell detailed stories, too. One such sculpture is the Sphinx (figure 60), regarded by many as the guardian of the pyramids of Giza, estimated over 5000 years old. It is commonly known that the Sphinx's nose along with the rest of its face had a distinctively African appearance and that French troops shot off the nose several decades ago. Many believe they did so to make the face look less African. Could the core significance of this ages-old structure contain the ancient memory of our original hybridization when everyone was African? Bear in mind that the Sphinx was built as one of the many forms of the sun god, Ra, who may well be the mythical representation of an extraterrestrial. As I'm sure you recall from earlier sections of this book, most ancient cultures' gods who roamed the skies were described in ways very reminiscent of extraterrestrials. According to Willis, among the many daily forms that Ra assumed, in the morning he was typically a scarab, which represented rebirth and transformation. Most of the other forms were human-animal hybrids, like that of the Sphinx. His evening form–the final stage of the forms that represented him–was a complete human wearing a double crown, normally only worn by kings.

My question is the following: Although birth, death, and regeneration are normally stated as the ideas behind Ra's phases, couldn't these various forms of Ra also be symbolic of man's transformation from an earlier hominid species to homo sapien? Think about it. The morning stage is the scarab, representing the beginning of man's transformation. The middle phases are mostly human-animal hybrid forms, representing the actual transformation process, entailing alien-human hybridization. In this middle process phase, the face of the Sphinx resembles the face of the hybrid being, which is African. The Sphinx's feline animal body represents Ra's divinity (extraterrestrial nature), as did animal bodies in many ancient cultures. The final phase of a completely human figure wearing crowns signifies that the hybridization process is finished and that the resulting being has superior qualities. In other words, he's now a modern man!

Other Sculptural Corroboration?

Similar sculptural indicators can be seen in the huge stone heads left by the ancient Olmecs in Mexico (figure 61). The Olmecs were the inhabitants of the once-mythical land of Olman on the coast of the Gulf of Mexico. According to Kolosimo (1973), Olman was said to be a place of ornately decorated buildings and sculptures, where silver and gold were in abundance, and where the residents wore elegant garments and fine jewelry. Olman's existence was finally confirmed with the discovery of its capital, a small island called La Venta, where the ruins of walls, edifices, and a central pyramid were found. The Olmec culture is estimated to have flourished between 1500 B.C. and 400 B.C. Why their culture disappeared so abruptly, is still a mystery, but they left behind their artifacts as a testimony to their lifestyle. The most significant of these artifacts are the stone carvings and sculptures that, like the Egyptian god Ra, depict various stages of human-animal hybrids. Interestingly enough, although several animal images (such as snakes) are a part of the pantheons of what is now Latin America, the Olmec stone motifs were mostly human-jaguar hybrids, which recalls the feline portion of the Sphinx. Also, like the god Ra, there is a form that is completely human. This form is depicted as faces on flat stone surfaces, as small human figures, and as colossal heads.

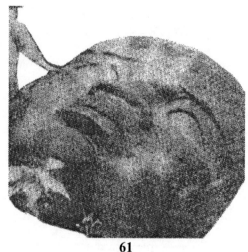

61

Even more interesting perhaps is the fact that, like the Sphinx, most of these human depictions, including the giant heads, have distinctly African facial features. Traces of jaguar qualities can be seen in such areas as the corners of the eyes, but, for the most part, the faces are unmistakably African. There are two versions of this head sprinkled around in various parts of Mexico. One has hair clearly braided in rows, typical of Africans. The other is wearing what looks like a space helmet (see figures 61, 62)! These massive stone heads weighing up to 24 tons each and standing over 6 feet high, were made of green serpentine marble and exhibit meticulously accurate detail—prodigious efforts that no one would have made to the honor or memory of ordinary people. Could these sculptures be likenesses of the first hybrid? And could their space helmets signify their alien side? By the way, the Olmecs taught that the human-jaguar beings were originally gods who came from the moon.

The Olmecs also influenced subsequent cultures in that region, including the Chorotegans and the Aztecs. Kolosimo (1973) notes that the Chorotegans, who live in what is now Nicaragua and northern Costa Rica also taught that the human-jaguars were beings of extraterrestrial origin and that they were responsible for the development of all human civilizations. Olmec influence is also evident in the motifs (including human-animal stone images) and style of the ruins of a famous city near Mexico City known by its Aztec name of Teotihuacan. According to regional myths, it was not built by humans, but by gods and god-human hybrids (demigods). Another very interesting aspect of Teotihuacan involves its most dominant architectural feature–its pyramids. These pyramids have certain similarities to the Olmecs and even more to the Great Pyramid (Cheops) at Giza, which is the largest of Egypt's seventy pyramids. For example, one of the pyramids is dedicated to the sun and has a base that measures 740 feet by 725 feet, which is identical to the base of the great Egyptian pyramid. The sun pyramid's height is 215 feet, which is exactly half of that of Cheops. Just more coincidences?

Just as the Olmecs influenced subsequent cultures, the once mythical city of Tiahuanaco is said to have influenced the Olmecs. It was discovered by explorers near Lake Titicaca in Bolivia and, according to Inca legend, was built by a family that had escaped a global catastrophe. Tiahuanaco culture was seen to have some of the same motifs and structures as that of the Olmecs. Among them, stone carvings of human-jaguar

62

hybrids and large pyramids! Contrary to earlier more conservative estimates, Tiahuanaco is said to be perhaps twice as old as the earliest Egyptian culture. Experts who examined the ruins of this harbor town, say the largest pyramid was still in the process of being built when it was suddenly and inexplicably abandoned along with the rest of the city. Some suggest a possible explanation by noting that the construction had abruptly stopped about 11,500 years ago–the time that Atlantis was destroyed, according to Plato's writings.

So where am I connecting the dots through all this? Here: The ancient cultures that I've mentioned in this section have very strong similarities in their cultures and myths; most notably, pyramids and stone images with varying degrees of human-animal mixtures, from half-and-half human-feline hybrids to completely human faces. These are cultures that impute divinity to their animal images, which supports the idea that these stone carvings reflect human-alien hybridization and that they involved the first humans, who were Africans. Ancient awareness that Africans were the first humans and hybrids can apparently be seen in the African features that are visible on the Sphinx, on Olmec sculptures, and some say even on the Mars Face. Whether or not the Mars Face actually has African features (see the Mars section in Chapter 6) is not really significant, because it still fits neatly into this group. After all, the mere fact that a giant humanoid face wearing an Egyptian headdress was carved in stone on Mars and positioned near a group of pyramids arranged like those in Egypt sounds a little too coincidental, wouldn't you say? And wouldn't you say that the common thread running through all these cultures and locations seems to be that of an extraterrestrial presence?

Other Evidence of Alien Intervention?

We've discussed a great deal about the alien presence among us from its beginnings to its ongoing status and its interventions in between. But are there any other strong trails that they've left through the centuries? Have our alien neighbors influenced in other visible ways that we haven't examined yet? Most definitely! Their influence can be seen at just about every point in our development. The trick is finding the often elusive evidence for it. After quite a bit of digging, I stumbled across several cases that I found quite interesting. Here are a couple of them:

Chariots of Gods or Demons?
The Incredible Truth About UFOs and Extraterrestrials

An Old Sparkplug?

On February 13, 1961, some peculiar-looking geodes were found in the mountains near Coso, California. One of the stones was sawed in half revealing a perfectly circular center composed of ceramic. This ceramic center contained a two-millimeter shaft made of light metal. The crusted stone on the object's outer surface was dated by expert geologists to be at least 500,000 years old, meaning, of course, that the ceramic device underneath was older. Further examination removed any remaining doubts that the object was artificially constructed and that it had some sort of electrical function! Comparisons with similar modern devices led to the speculation that it might have served as a kind of spark plug. But who or what had the knowledge to build such a thing over 500,000 years ago? And for what? The who has to be someone taught by extraterrestrials. The next section might yield a possible clue to the what.

Ancient Airplanes?

Among its collection of golden artifacts, the Banco de Colombia has a an object that bears a striking resemblance to a modern delta-winged jet airplane (see figure 63). What makes it so unusual is that it's at least 1000 years old and probably much older! Most observers had automatically assumed that the object was intended to be a fish or a flying insect and that the similarity to a jet plane was purely coincidental. But then the object caught the eye of a number of experts who began to question this assumption. The most notable of these experts, according to Charles Berlitz (1973), was Dr. Ivan Sanderson, an archaeologist and biologist. He noticed that the model includes important details not present on fish and insects. For example, the edges of the delta-shaped wings are equipped with what looked like ailerons or elevators, standard equipment on jets. The tail of the object, unlike the upright position of a fish's tail, is flanged like the tails of modern planes. Furthermore, there is an indentation at the position where a plane's cockpit would normally be.

63

Another expert, J.A. Ulrich, engineer and former fighter pilot, upon seeing the model for the first time and closely scrutinizing it, insisted that it was a model of an F-102 fighter jet. His certainty was based on such details as the slight downward curve of the end of the wings, which is required for aircraft with "super-power abrupt rise." In addition, he remarked that the model's rudder was standard on planes and that what Sanderson had thought were elevators might be speed brakes. So, does this object just coincidentally have the look and features of a modern jet plane? Not likely. There are just too many variables involved. But who built it and why? The most likely scenarios are that extraterrestrials either built it for themselves or provided the technology to humans to build it. I would lean towards the latter, since it was designed for travel in Earth's airspaces.

A Mechanical Starfinder

In 1900 during a dive off the coast of Greece, sponge divers discovered a ship that had sunk near the southern island of Kythera in about 100 B.C. The statues, vases, and other artifacts salvaged from the wreckage were handed over to archaeologists. While searching through the various objects, they noticed a strange-looking corroded piece of bronze that was flat and resembled a broken section of a large circular dish. After cleaning and closely inspecting it, they saw that it was part of a complicated mechanical device that gave highly accurate astronomical information regarding the positioning and movement of the moon and the stars (see figure 64). According to von Daeniken (1973), it was driven by complex gears consisting of "about forty cog wheels, nine adjustable scales, and three axes." The instructions inscribed on the object are in Greek, but experts agree that the Greeks at that time had no such technology. They also acknowledged that no one in the world at that time was supposed to have it, and thus were at a loss to explain its existence. Is this another instance where extraterrestrials intervened technologically in our development?

64

(Photocopy of ancient computer found off the island coast of Kyhtera)

Electricity in Ancient Times?

Like ninety nine percent of the world, you most likely believe that the use of electricity is a relatively recent phenomenon, right? I did, too, until I saw an excerpt from an ancient Indian document preserved in the Indian Prince's Library at Ujjain. It's called the *Agastya Samhita* and contains instructions for making electrical batteries! Tomas provided the translated excerpt as follows:

"Place a well-cleaned copper plate in an earthenware vessel. Cover it first by copper sulphate and then by moist sawdust. After that put a mercury-amalgamated-zinc sheet on top of the sawdust to avoid polarization. The contact will produce an energy known by the twin name of Mitra-Varuna. Water will be split by this current into Pranavayu and Udanavayu. A chain of one hundred jars is said to give a very active and effective force."

As Tomas further explains, we now know the *Mitra-Varuna* as a cathode-anode and the *Pranavayu* and *Udanavayu* as oxygen and hydrogen, respectively. These instructions, plus discoveries of "perpetually-burning" lamps in several Indian temples as well as those of the Nagas (serpent deities who live underground near the Himalayas) give further credence to the now obvious evidence that electricity was used by ancient people. Again the main question is how this knowledge was passed on to humans. More extraterrestrial influence?

Atomic Weapons in The Distant Past?

There are strong indications that extraterrestrials brought something far more destructive than aircraft and electricity to the ancient world–atomic weapons! We have already discussed the possibility that the Old Testament story of Sodom and Gomorrah's destruction may have involved an atomic weapon. Ancient Indian texts offer even stronger evidence that atomic weapons were used in the distant past. Tomas notes that the *Mausola Parva* describes weapons that sound like modern nuclear missiles or bombs. These "thunderbolts" and "gigantic messengers of death" were said to reduce entire armies to ashes and cause the nails and hair of the survivors to fall out. It also poisoned food, shattered pottery and made birds turn white. One might think at first glance that this was a picture of Hiroshima towards the end of World War II.

The sacred Indian writings in the *Drona Parva* provided even more detail: "A blazing missile possessed of the radiance of smokeless fire was discharged. A thick gloom suddenly encompassed the heavens. Clouds roared into the higher air (mushroom clouds?), showering blood. The world, scorched by the heat of that weapon, seemed to be in fever." It was further described as a *flare-up of ten thousand suns*. Is there tangible evidence that atomic weapons might have been used in the distant past? What about a radioactive skeleton in the region referred to in the texts? That's right. A radioactive skeleton has been discovered in India! The level of its radioactivity was fifty times higher than normal!

A good question is whether humans had access to these weapons of mass destruction or whether only aliens used them. If humans had used them, they were most likely part of an advanced civilization that had benefitted from alien technological intervention. Perhaps a place like Atlantis. If aliens had used them, a possible reason why might be intervention to halt dangerous forms of corruption as may have existed, for example, in Sodom and Gomorrah. Or maybe some human military threat or conflict had grown so great that aliens had to use atomic weapons to stop it. Who used them is less significant, of course, than the fact that they were used at all in the ancient past.

Testimony by The Palenque Relief?

An ancient stone relief representing the god Kukulcan was found in Palenque, Mexico, in 1935. Many ufologists insist that it depicts Kukulcan as an astronaut manipulating controls in a space ship of some type. Erich von Daeniken said the following about the relief:

"There sits a human being with the upper part of his body bent forward like a racing motorcyclist; today any child would identify his vehicle as a rocket. It is pointed at the front, then changes to strangely grooved indentations like inlet ports, widens out, and terminates at the tail in a darting flame. The crouching being himself is manipulating a number of indefinable controls and has the heel of his left foot on a kind of pedal. His clothing is appropriate: short trousers with a broad belt, a jacket with a modern Japanese opening at the neck, and closely fitting bands at arms and legs. With our knowledge of similar pictures, we should be surprised if the complicated headgear were missing. And there it is with the usual indentations and tubes, and something like antennae on top. Our space traveler–he is clearly depicted as one–is not only bent forward tensely; he is also looking intently at an apparatus hanging in front of this face. The astronaut's front seat is separated by struts from the rear portion of the vehicle, in which symmetrically arranged boxes, circles, points, and spirals can be seen." (Von Daeniken, 1971)

Is it a depiction of an astronaut manipulating the controls of his ship? There are, of course supporters and detractors of this notion. Observe the artistic reproduction of the relief in figure 65 below and judge for yourself.

65
(The Palenque relief)

Personal Alien Visits?

An inevitable question is, if aliens are so involved in and concerned about our development, why haven't they contacted our world leaders. Well, actually some people think that they have. These people have provided documentary evidence that strongly suggests that extraterrestrials have contacted world leaders all throughout history, predictably in times of military threats and conflicts. These visitors have had various external appearances, including brown, red, and grayish skin color. Their purpose for the visits have apparently been to influence the important decisions the leaders needed to make, in particular, to attempt to dissuade them from military aggression. Interestingly, the visitors often make predictions about the leaders' lives and actions that come true. This, of course, suggests that some extraterrestrials may have extrasensory abilities. As I mentioned in Chapter I, there are many sightings reports that tell of aliens with such abilities. The following are three of the more notable instances of apparent alien visitations:

James Edward Gilmer

To Adolf Hitler?

66

Hermann Rauschning, who was Governor of Danzig during Adolf Hitler's Third Reich, related that the Fuehrer had spoken to him of a red-skinned man who had visited him several times and told him that he was a member of a race of beings who dwelt in a subterranean city and were technologically far ahead of surface-dwellers, according to author Brad Steiger (1973). Among Hitler's statements about the being, he was reportedly quoted as saying, "The new man is living amongst us now! He is here!... I was afraid of him." Who could have made Adolf Hitler afraid? Certainly no ordinary person. The visitor reportedly cautioned Hitler about the possible consequences of pursuing his military plans. Those consequences included Hitler's own demise. Did these visitations trigger the Nazi search an underground alien civilization (Chapter 7)?

To Napoleon Bonaparte?

67

A red-skinned man also appeared to French ruler Napoleon Bonaparte several times during his military campaigns, according to Steiger. The strange being warned Bonaparte of the dangers of his aggressive military campaigns and told him that he had given such warnings to rulers in the past. The visitor told him further that the French people were becoming increasingly fearful of his ambitions. He predicted that, even though the ruler's campaign in Egypt had begun auspiciously with the battle of the Pyramids, Napoleon's Egyptian plans would ultimately fail, and he would return to France to find her surrounded by England, Russia, Turkey, and an allied Europe. Moreover, the being predicted that Parisian mobs would confront him in anger over his actions. Sure enough, the predictions came true. He appeared only once more–shortly prior to Napoleon's abdication. On that morning, the stranger was said to have approached Counselor of State Mole for permission to see the emperor. Mole had been given orders that no one could see him, so he declined. But when Mole went in and described the man to Napoleon, he was told to show him in immediately. If the red man was an illusion, could Counselor Mole have shared it?

To Charles XII?

Charles XII of Sweden was also reportedly paid a visit by a strange man. As Steiger recounts, this visitor was reportedly small and had grayish skin. The mysterious stranger had repeatedly warned the king to cease his incessant military campaigns not only for the safety of others, but for his own as well. But Charles stubbornly refused to do so. Finally, in 1718, during the battle of Fredrikshald, he succumbed to a mortal head wound. Just a coincidence? Who's to say if these visitations actually happened. There is certainly no concrete proof that they did. The question remains, however, that, if they were illusions, how did the aliens' predictions come true? Another intriguing question is whether or not the strangers actually demonstrated extrasensory abilities or whether they (or other members of their race) physically intervened to bring about what they had predicted.

Chapter 9

The Government's UFO Coverups

Given the sheer weight of unexplainable sightings and the behavior of the U.S. government during its so-called UFO investigations, the question is no longer whether our government is aware of the existence of UFOs, but why it is covering up what it knows. There is ample evidence that the government has suppressed its knowledge of UFOs and waged a continuous campaign to dissuade the public from believing its own eyes.

Passive Coverups

The first indications of an official coverup occurred during World War II, with the enigmatic foo fighters. After realizing that they were not weapons of enemy nations, as several governments had initially believed, we fell officially silent once we began suspecting what they really were. This silence persisted, despite the fact that sightings reports continued after World War II and rose sharply in 1947.

It was apparently because UFOs had not yet captured our collective imagination that the government's coverup had been a more passive one. As you recall, the public's interest in flying saucers began catching fire in 1947 after the Kenneth Arnold sighting. When it did, the government could no longer keep quiet about it. Thus, with the very next high profile sighting–the Roswell crash—the active coverups began; that is, the government began actively feeding the public misinformation about UFOs, and continues to do so today. Let's take a brief look at the evolution of coverups in this country, focusing primarily on some of the more significant official UFO investigations.

The Beginning of Active Coverups

A Review of the Roswell Coverup

As you recall from Chapter 4, immediately after the recovery of the wreckage, the active coverup had still not yet been put into place. The military openly issued a press statement announcing the recovery of UFO wreckage. Shortly thereafter, however, Washington officials investigating the crash reportedly began ordering complete silence about it, using direct and indirect threats. Even high-ranking military personnel were cast into dark about the situation. After being assigned to oversee the air transport of the wreckage to Wright Field (later called Wright-Patterson) in Ohio, Major Jesse Marcel was ordered back to Roswell after an interim stop with the wreckage at Carswell Air Base in Fort Worth, Texas. After sending the UFO debris on to Wright Field, the Commander of the 8th Army Air Force at Carswell, Brigadier General Roger Ramey, issued another press statement retracting the earlier one about the recovered saucer and claiming that the wreckage was actually pieces of a weather balloon. This was the start of an active coverup campaign that is still underway.

The Secret Arctic Operation

Shortly after the Roswell crash, Lieutenant Colonel Wendel Stevens was put in charge of a secret operation to gather information about UFOs reportedly sighted over the Arctic. He also oversaw the installation and dismantling of special video and audio equipment to record UFO sightings. Sure enough, once in the Arctic, his team began spotting UFO activity which continued almost daily until the end of the mission. Once the audio and video recordings were packed and secured, they were escorted in secrecy to Washington, D.C., and not even Stevens was allowed to look at them or acknowledge their existence again. (Fawcett)

Majestic-12

At the end of 1984, a roll of film was delivered to television producer Jamie Shandera by an unknown sender. It showed classified documents about a highly secret organization referred to as Majestic-12, MJ-12, and Majic, that was established in 1947 by President Truman in reaction to the Roswell crash. Its mission was to further explore what happened at Roswell, to research subsequent UFO phenomena, and to report all findings directly to the President. According to Timothy Good, a copy of such an MJ-12 report dated 18 November 1952 and addressed to President-elect Eisenhower was discovered and included the statement that the "remains of four alien bodies from the Roswell wreckage were recovered (see figure 83)." Furthermore it named the twelve members of Majestic-12, who turned out to be very prestigious high-ranking officials (See figure 82). The following is a list of their names and brief descriptions:

1) *Dr. Lloyd Berkner*, a scientist working for the Joint Research and Development Board; 2) *Dr. Detlev Bronk*, a famous physiologist and biophysicist who chaired the National Research Council and was a Medical Advisory Board member of the Atomic Energy Commission; 3) *Dr. Vannevar Bush* (figure 68), a highly respected scientist who organized, among other things, the Office of Scientific Research and Development in 1943, which led to the Manhattan Project for the development of the first atomic bomb; 4) *James Forrestal* (figure

69), former Secretary of the Navy and Secretary of Defense (at the time of the Roswell crash); 5) *Gordon Gray*, Assistant Secretary of the Army, at the time MJ-12 was established; 6) *Vice-Admiral Roscoe Hillenkoetter* (figure 70), Director of Central Intelligence (DCI) at the time of the Roswell Crash and first CIA Director; 7) *Dr. Jerome Hunsaker*, designed aircraft, headed two departments at the Massachusetts Institute of Technology, and chaired the National Advisory Committee for Aeronautics; 8) *Dr. Donald Menzel* directed Harvard's observatory and was involved with the National Security Agency where he held a Top Secret Ultra security clearance; 9) *General Robert Montague*, Base Commander of the Atomic Energy Commission installation at Sandia Base in Albuquerque, New Mexico at the time of the Roswell crash; 10) *Rear Admiral Sidney Souers*, served as first DCI (1946) and Executive Secretary of the National Security Council at the time of the Roswell crash; 11) *General Nathan Twining* (figure 71), commanded overseas bombing operations during World War II and headed the Air Materiel Command (AMC) at Wright Field (now Wright-Patterson Air Force Base). Shortly after the Roswell crash, he revealed that the AMC had concluded, following its study of the crash, that the wreckage was extraterrestrial in origin! 12) *General Hoyt Vandenburg* (figure 72), second DCI.

68
(Bush)

69
(Forrestal)

70
(Hillenkoeter)

71
(Twining)

72
(Vandenburg)

The government continues to deny the existence of Majestic-12, of course, even though several MJ-12 documents have been discovered (figures 82, 83). Were all those documents faked? The members have all passed away now, but they were certainly real people whose existence has been verified.

Project Sign

Yet another government project established in the wake of the Roswell crash was Project Sign. It was headquartered at Wright Field and under the command of the AMC's Technical Intelligence Division. Its mission, according to David Jacobs, was to collect and evaluate all possible information regarding UFO sightings, to determine whether the UFOs are a threat to national security, and to report the information and conclusions to appropriate government agencies. Publicly referred to as Project Saucer, Project Sign was created at the end of 1947 and commenced its work at the beginning of 1948.

Project Sign's establishment increased in priority because of a famous UFO sighting that had preceded it by two weeks–that of Captain Thomas Mantell (Chapter 4). Sensationalized in the press, this high-profile case had accelerated the rise in the public's interest in UFOs and offered yet another challenge to the government's attempts to explain away such incidents. While carrying out thorough investigations of reported sightings, Project Sign personnel were reportedly instructed to do their best to explain as secret foreign weapons the UFOs that they couldn't dismiss as conventional aircraft or natural phenomena. According to Jacobs, they even consulted German weapons experts in the United States for their opinions on the possibility that the objects could be Soviet weapons made from German designs. The Germans said no.

Within the first few months, the group had encountered so many unexplainable cases that they began writing their reports almost exclusively from the perspective that UFOs were a real phenomenon of extraterrestrial origin. Using the group's findings, the AMC wrote a top secret "Estimate of the Situation," a report on its assessment of all UFO sightings since the ghost rockets. The gist of the AMC's opinion was that the evidence showed that UFOs were indeed extraterrestrial phenomena. Apparently not pleased with this growing body of reports confirming the existence of UFOs and apprehensive of such information leaking to the public, top-level Air Force officials replaced Project Sign personnel with others who would write UFO reports for public consumption, based on the notion that all UFOs reports were hoaxes, hallucinations, or misidentifications. To complete this change in approach, Project Sign was terminated at the end of the year and replaced by another project–Project Grudge. (Fawcett)

Project Grudge

In a sense, Project Grudge was just another name for Project Sign, but with a different approach to studying UFOs. Like Project Sign, its mission was to collect and evaluate reports of UFO sightings. But instead of carrying out consistently objective evaluations as Project Sign had done, Project Grudge dismissed out of hand phenomena that could not be shown to be hoax, hallucination, or misidentification. And unlike Project Sign, Project Grudge leaked information to the public about its research and indicated that it had never encountered anything of an extraterrestrial nature.

Project Grudge occasionally twisted the facts surrounding unexplainable phenomena to make them look explainable. One instance of this, as Jacobs notes, involves a report filed by a T-6 training pilot. As he was preparing to land, he noticed an unusual light, and moved closer to get a better look at it. As he did, the object suddenly climbed to a position above his plane. He continued trying to get a better angle to observe it, but it kept maneuvering out of position for him, sometimes executing impossible sharp angle turns. It seemed to be toying with him. Finally, just before giving up, it remained still long enough for him to see that it was a "dark gray and oval-shaped" object, which then shot off towards the coast. The pilot's report was corroborated by four Air Force witnesses who had watched the incredible scene from the ground. Nonetheless, Project Grudge was ordered to state that the object was nothing more than a weather balloon! The active coverup was in full swing.

Despite Project Grudge's twisting and denying the truth, public interest in UFOs continued to grow unabated. The project's staff began to fear that, despite its misinformation tactics, the very existence of an official Air Force organization dedicated solely to the investigation of UFOs probably stoked people's belief in UFOs more than dampened it. At first the project's operations were drastically curtailed. Seeing that this had no affect on the public, the Air Force stated that continuing the project was a waste of time and money and officially terminated Project Grudge at the end of 1949. (Fawcett)

Project Blue Book

Actually Project Grudge wasn't completely dead in 1949. That announcement was for the public. It had slowed down operationally to a nearly dormant state, but was still functional. In 1952, the Air Force decided to change Grudge from an Air Force organization to an independent one, giving it the official title of Aerial Phenomena Group under the code name Project Blue Book. Because of their independence, Project Blue Book personnel didn't have to go through the normal chain of command to obtain sightings reports from the Air Force and Army bases around the world. It also left very few stones unturned as far as other sources of sightings reports, garnering them from practically anyone and anywhere, including meteorologists, private pilots, and ordinary people who just happen to spot a UFO.

The advent of Blue Book also marked another chapter in the government's relationship with the press. First of all, while the Air Force did not mention Blue Book by name, it admitted that it still examined UFO sightings that couldn't be explained. On this basis, according to Jacobs, the Air Force agreed to replace its press policy of "no comment" with one that provided as much explanation as possible of the government's position on a particular sighting report. Of course, the "explanations" continued to consist of turning as many unexplainable sightings as possible into hoaxes, hallucinations, and misidentifications. (Fawcett)

In 1966, under pressure of growing criticism of Project Blue Book, the Air Force commissioned the University of Colorado to carry out an independent scientific UFO study that was issued in 1968. It is known as the Condon Report. It concluded that further government UFO studies were unjustified for lack of evidence. A torrent of criticism rained on the report, charging, among other things, that the study was inconsistent in its treatment of the cases it studied and failed to properly address sightings that it couldn't explain. (World Almanac)

Finally, at the end of 1969, after twenty two years, the Air Force officially terminated its investigation of UFOs. It justified its decision by the Condon Report, arguing that, since Project Blue Book had not yielded any results that could be seen as evidence for the existence of extraterrestrials, any further UFO studies would be a waste of time, money, and effort, and that neither science nor national security would be served by continuing them. Of course, we know that the government's UFO investigations did not really end with Project Blue Book. Neither did its campaign of misinforming the public about UFOs, or its coverup of mountains of evidence that prove the existence of alien visitors.

NATO Coverups

It goes without saying that our government is not the only one involved in UFO coverups. Many other governments, especially the highly industrialized ones, have been doing basically the same things as ours in terms of misleading the public. While it is not within the scope of this book to focus on the activities of other governments, a brief example can be seen in the coverups the North Atlantic Treaty Organization (NATO). An extension of the 1948 Brussels Treaty for military cooperation, NATO comprises the United States, England, France, Italy, Belgium, Luxembourg, Denmark, Canada, Portugal, Turkey, Spain, Greece, Iceland, Norway, the Netherlands, and Germany. These sixteen countries have actively participated in the coverup of many UFO sightings and encounters.

Examples of the coverups are the NATO sightings mentioned in Chapter 4, which have never been publicly acknowledged as true by NATO officials. In addition to pacing NATO exercises, UFOs have been spotted by NATO eyewitnesses and radar flying over Europe, and over the Supreme Headquarters Allied Powers Europe (SHAPE), which is NATO's headquarters. Unnamed sources inside NATO have revealed that SHAPE has written several reports on these encounters, which remain classified. Another classified fact about NATO coverups that has been leaked is NATO's three-year study of the unidentified objects frequently spotted overhead. The study was classified "Cosmic Top Secret" which is NATO highest possible classification. According to inside sources, the report concluded that UFOs were real extraterrestrial vehicles and that to publicly reveal the truth about them could be very "disruptive" for mankind unless it is properly prepared for it.

Area 51 Revealed

It has been known since the Roswell crash that Wright-Patterson Air Force Base has served as a storage and examination area for alien crash debris and bodies. Only relatively recently, however, have we seen irrefutable proof of the existence of a government installation in Nevada known officially as Area 51, but also as Dreamland and Groom Lake. See an excerpt from a *Baltimore Sun* article on Area 51 in figure 73 and a Russian satellite photo in 74.

Located 85 miles north-northwest of Las Vegas, near Nellis Air Force Base, and with a runway almost six miles long, Area 51 was continuously dismissed by the government as the stuff of storytellers. Then Russian satellite photos of the installation were obtained and published (see press article in figure 72 and Russian satellite photo in figure 73), prompting the government to quietly retract its earlier denials. Now that the government has admitted that it lied about the existence of Area 51, what are we to believe about government denials of its activities at Area 51? Are we to continue to believe government denials that Area 51 scientists are

Aerial photos reveal Area 51

[*Area, from Page 1F*]

above the site is restricted, few accurate photos of the region exist.

"If you fly anywhere near the place, they threaten to shoot you down," Andrus says. The only previous pictures have been fuzzy, but on this new set — taken with state-of-the-art equipment and posted on Aerial Images' Web site (www.terraserver.com, which was overwhelmed by visitors yesterday) — "you can make out airstrips, antennas, buildings and a number of unpaved roads."

73

not only developing and testing new conventional aircraft designs, but also various types of devices based on the reverse engineering of UFOs recovered from crash sites (see section below on Colonel Corso)?!. Leaks of such activities have been so frequent, that the state of Nevada has named a road near the installation "Extraterrestrial Highway."

74

Government Sources Confirm The Reality of UFOs

Through the years since the Roswell crash, we have seen and heard evidence from within the government that UFOs are a real phenomenon. This evidence takes various forms, from documentary evidence to sworn testimonies by government officials involved in UFO investigations. Let's glance briefly at a few of them.

Major Jesse Marcel

75

As you recall from the Roswell crash, Major Jesse Marcel was an intelligence officer at the 509th Bomb Group at Roswell Army Air Field who was part of the crash investigation. After the military had released a press statement describing the object as a flying saucer, Marcel was assigned to head a team that was to fly the wreckage to Wright Field for examination. Upon making an interim stop at Carswell Air Base in Fort Worth, Texas, he was relieved of his assignment by the Commander of the 8th Army Air Force, Brigadier General Roger Ramey, warned with indirect threats to keep quiet about the crash, and ordered back to Roswell. After sending the UFO debris on to

Wright Field, Ramey called a press conference, changed the earlier story by saying that the wreckage was actually from a weather balloon, and presented pieces of a weather balloon as proof.

Marcel went along with the coverup for years out of fear, but finally went public with his story, divulging that the pieces of the "weather balloon" were indeed parts of a crashed UFO and that the bodies of small humanoid creatures had also been retrieved from the crash site and sent to Wright Field for examination and storage. Figure 76 is a drawing of the face of one of the aliens reportedly described by a military nurse who claimed to have seen the bodies retrieved from the Roswell crash.

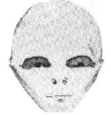

76

Dr. J. Allen Hynek

77

Dr. Hynek was the scientific advisor for Project Blue Book for its entire duration (1952-1969). Throughout the seventeen years of sightings that he helped to evaluate, he dutifully abided by the government's order to find creative ways to convince the public that none of the sightings were ever alien spacecraft, but rather explainable things like swamp gas, weather balloons, temperature inversions, conventional aircraft, hallucinations, hoaxes, and other things. In 1973, amazingly, he founded the Center for UFO Studies. Why would a scientist who had just spent seventeen years of his life disproving the existence of UFOs create a center to study them? The answer came a few years later. Shortly before his death in 1985, when he had nothing more to fear from the government, Hynek bared his soul publicly about the lie he had been forced to tell for so long. He admitted that UFOs were real and that the government had deceived the public in order to avoid the disturbing effect that the truth would have on it. (Reader's Digest)

Robert Dean

A former intelligence analyst at NATO's SHAPE headquarters, Robert Dean recently announced on public television that he had read a report on UFOs written by SHAPE in the early 1960s and classified Cosmic Top Secret. According to Dean, the report clearly asserted that UFOs were a real alien phenomenon.

Chariots of Gods or Demons?
The Incredible Truth About UFOs and Extraterrestrials

Admiral Roscoe Hillenkoetter

On 28 February 1960, the first Director of Central Intelligence, who was also the first CIA Director and an MJ-12 member, Admiral Roscoe Hillenkoeter, publicly confessed that he was part of an ongoing government campaign to conceal the truth about UFOs. He indicated that they were real and called on the government to be honest with the public.

78

Colonel Phillip J. Corso

79

Publicly, he served on President Eisenhower's National Security Council and headed the Foreign Technology Desk in the Army's Research and Development Department, but Colonel Phillip J. Corso also worked behind the scenes in the Army's secret UFO activities which he described in his book, *The Day After Roswell*. In the book, he cites evidence that proves that the object that crashed near Roswell was a UFO and that the government has gone to great lengths to hide the truth about this and other notable UFO encounters. He recounts how he was present during the "dismantling and appropriation" of the Roswell UFO and startles the public by claiming that he had directed a government reverse engineering project that has saturated industries (clandestinely) with UFO technology, leading to such things as integrated circuit chips, fiber optics, lasers, and stealth technology.

Astronaut Edgar Mitchell

Several years ago, after Apollo 14 Astronaut Edgar Mitchell had publicly announced his conviction that UFOs were real, he was asked how the government had managed to keep the reality of UFOs such a secret for so long. He responded that the secret hasn't been kept. He pointed to the many leaks, including his own, that have exposed the government's lies and coverups, and have thus severely weakened its credibility in this issue.

James Edward Gilmer

An Air Force Textbook

Interestingly enough, the most damning evidence proving the government's awareness of the reality of UFOs may not come from the mouths of government officials, but rather from the pages of a government textbook. In 1968 the Air Force's space science textbook was found to contain several sections that taught that UFOs were real extraterrestrial phenomena! As Fowler (1974) notes, one of the textbook's early passages on UFOs reads:

"The most stimulating theory for us is that UFOs are material objects which are either manned or remote-controlled by beings who are alien to this planet. There is some evidence supporting this viewpoint."

Another textbook passage describes the *average alien:*

"The most commonly described alien is about three and one-half feet tall, has a round head (helmet?), arms reaching to or below his knees, and is wearing a silvery space suit or coveralls. Other aliens appear to be essentially the same as earthmen, while still others have particularly wide (wrap-around) eyes and mouths with very thin lips…"

The textbook's concluding section on UFOs is especially revealing:

"The data…suggest the existence of at least three and maybe four different groups of aliens (possibly at different stages of development). This…implies the existence of intelligent life on a majority of the planets in our solar system, or a surprisingly strong interest in Earth by members of other solar systems."

Clearly, this shakes the very foundation of the government's position of denial. How can it continue to tell the public that UFOs don't exist while teaching its own officials that they do?

Does Our Government Have an Agreement With Aliens?

It's clear now that our government knows that extraterrestrials exist and that they have subterranean and/or submarine bases on Earth as well as on other bodies in our solar system. Has this knowledge led to any kind of agreement with them? Quite possibly. The government could have some type of agreement with aliens that allows them to continue their mission with certain stipulations. But that would imply that we've communicated with them, you say? Naturally. Is that so hard to believe? After so many millenia of involvement with humans, aliens have most likely developed various ways of communicating with us. Perhaps through electronic signals, telepathy, or even personal contact. We've already seen possible examples of personal alien contact with world leaders (chapter 8). But could aliens really meet with us without being conspicuous? Sure! As we have seen in many sightings reports, the appearance of aliens can vary any where from *very alien* to *very human*, meaning that aliens have probably subjected some of their own groups to alien-human genetic mingling. Perhaps they did so to interface and communicate more easily with humans.

A *deep throat* recently stated that the government has indeed reached an agreement with aliens allowing them to maintain their subterranean/submarine bases and to continue their mission in our spaces without our interference as long as they refrain from further mingling in our societies or any other activities that could be considered disruptive to our way of life.

What's my personal view on this? Although I thought it useful to mention these possible scenarios, I don't believe that our government (or any other government on earth) has an agreement with aliens at this time. I think it's possible that aliens have secretly contacted private citizens or even leaders during the modern UFO era, but I have seen no corroborating evidence or any other compelling reasons to believe that such contact has resulted in an agreement of any type. In fact, I've seen evidence to the contrary; namely, the fact that our fighter jets (and those of other countries) still occasionally pursue and even fire on UFOs. I rather tend to believe that, if anything at all, we might have a tacit and tenuous live-and-let-live understanding with them, based loosely on the assumption that they will understand from our aggressive behavior toward them that they should stay out of sight. Perhaps chasing and firing on them at times, is our crude way of reminding them of such an understanding, if it exists.

I do believe, however, that, at some point in the future, a cooperative arrangement with them is very likely. Once the government officially tells us that they exist, our collective intellectual curiosity, if nothing else, will start the ball rolling toward official contact with them. And, who knows? Perhaps our alien neighbors will somehow know when we are ready for that next step in our relations.

Reasons for Government Coverups

All the possible reasons I've heard for UFO coverups thus far involve fear– the government's and the public's. More specifically, the government fears the possible forms and consequences of the public's reactions to being officially told that we share our planet with extraterrestrials. The most feared public reaction would be widespread panic. Anarchic and destructive panic. The kind reflected to an extent in the famous Martian incident of 1938 when Orson Welles's mock radio newscast of a Martian invasion caused real terror and chaos among listeners.

Another possible fear-based reaction is harmful and even deadly violence. The kind of violence that humans are often known to resort to when we encounter new types of people and creatures that we don't understand. As Fowler points out, the Air Force's 1968 space science textbook provides a number of excellent examples of the government's thinking along these lines. In a section entitled "Human Fear and Hostility," the government cites our xenophobic reactions as a reason to continue to keep us in the dark about UFOs. The following is an excerpt.

"Contacting humans is downright dangerous. Think about that for a moment! On the microscopic level our bodies reject and fight (through production antibodies) any alien material; this process helps us fight off disease, but it also sometimes results in allergenic reactions to innocuous materials. On the macroscopic (psychological and sociological) level we are antagonistic to beings that are "different." For proof of that, just watch how an odd child is treated by other children, or how a minority group is treated by other children, or how a minority group is socially deprived, or how the Arabs feel about the Israelis (Chinese vs Japanese, Turks vs Greeks, etc.). In case you are hesitant to extend that concept to the treatment of aliens, let me point out that in very ancient times, possible extraterrestrials may have been treated as gods, but in the last two thousand years, the evidence is that any possible aliens have been ripped apart by mobs, shot and shot at, physically assaulted......and in general treated with fear and aggression. In Ireland about 1,000 A.D., supposed airships were treated as "demon-ships." In Lyons, France, "admitted" space travelers were killed (840 A.D.)."

The textbook describes more instances of what the government considers our trigger-happy inclinations with the unfamiliar, especially when it involves something uncontrollable, like UFOs:

"More recently, on 24 July 1957, Russian anti-aircraft batteries on the Kouril Islands opened fire on UFOs. Although all Soviet anti-aircraft batteries on the Islands were in action, no hits were made. The UFOs were luminous and moved very fast. We too have fired on UFOs. About ten o'clock one morning, a radar site near a fighter base picked up a UFO doing 700 mph. The UFO then slowed to 100 mph, and two F-86's were scrambled to intercept. Eventually, one F-86 closed on the UFO at about 3,000 feet altitude. The UFO began to accelerate away but the pilot still managed to get within 500 yards of the target for a short period of time. It was definitely saucer-shaped. As the pilot pushed the F-86 at top speed, the UFO began to pull away. When the range reached 1,000 yards, the pilot armed his guns and fired in an attempt to down the saucer. He failed, and the UFO pulled away rapidly, vanishing in the distance."

The Air Force textbook cites yet another case of human aggression against UFOs, but this time against the occupants themselves:

"On Sunday evening, 21 August 1955, eight adults and three children were on the Sutton Farm (one-half mile from Kelly, Kentucky) when, according to them, one of the children saw a brightly glowing UFO settle behind the barn, out of sight from where he stood. Other witnesses on nearby farms also saw the object. However, the Suttons dismissed it as a "shooting star," and did not investigate. Approximately thirty minutes later (at 8 P.M.), the family dogs began barking so two of the men went to the back door and looked out. Approximately 50 feet away and coming toward them was a creature wearing a glowing silvery suit. It was about three and one-half feet tall with a large round head and very long arms. It had large webbed hands which were equipped with claws. The two Suttons grabbed a twelve-gauge shotgun and a 22-caliber pistol, and fired at close range. They could hear the pellets and bullets ricochet as if off of metal. The creature was knocked down, but jumped up and scrambled away. The Suttons retreated into the house, turned off all inside lights, and turned on the porch light. At that moment, one of the women who was peeking out of the dining room window discovered that a creature with some sort of helmet and wide slit eyes was peeking back at her. She screamed, the men rushed in and started shooting. The creature was knocked backwards but again scrambled away without apparent harm. More shooting occurred (a total of about 50 rounds) over the next 20 minutes and the creatures finally left (perhaps feeling unwelcome?). After a two-hour wait (for safety), the Suttons left too. By the time the police got there, the aliens were gone but the Suttons would not move back to the farm. They sold it and departed. This reported incident does bear out the contention though that humans are dangerous..."

While it's certainly true that we humans are generally xenophobic and that we sometimes shoot first and ask questions later when confronted by things we don't understand or control, it's also true that we are extremely adaptable creatures and that we learn to understand things over time. And understanding something makes us feel safer with it. In ancient times, some primitive groups used to believe that thunderstorms signaled the anger of the gods. While we can't physically control thunderstorms now any more than we did then, we feel safer in their presence because we understand them more. We can predict their occurrence and behavior and we know to relate to them in terms of preparations and what to do and not to do in their presence. We have grown to accept them as natural parts of our lives. And I feel that, given time, we will come to accept extraterrestrials as part of our lives. Therefore, I reject the government's fear-related arguments for continuing its coverups.

Chapter 10

How The Truth About UFOs Could Impact Our Lives

The Implications

If and when the government finally divulges the truth about UFOs, the impact on our lives will be deep and far-reaching, although less so for people who already know that they exist. After we recover from the initial shock, we'll have to integrate this new concept into our reality. Then we'll have to make corresponding adjustments in the affected areas of our lives, which will be difficult and even painful for some of us. But, again, for some individuals and institutions, knowing about UFOs beforehand would soften and shorten–if not eliminate—this adjustment period. The main question that surfaces on this issue is, naturally, which areas of our lives will likely be affected the most. I think it goes without saying that our intellectual, social, and spiritual/religious lives would be among those most affected, both personally and institutionally. Let's take a look at some of the possible scenarios.

The Intellectual Impact

Integrating the concept of UFOs into our intellectual lives is not just a matter of mentally accepting it. That's just the beginning. The institutions traditionally involved in our intellectual lives, especially our educational institutions, will also have to adjust, and that's where most of the difficulties will emerge. Time-honored facts and assumptions about us and our universe will have to be purged and replaced by new ones. Our most eminent scientists and educators will have to admit that their theories and teachings were based on false premises. The long list of changes that will appear in revised textbooks will seem daunting at first, but, with time, will become just another normal part of our curriculae. Here are a few of the items on that list:

1) Earth will no longer be considered the only planet where intelligent life developed.
2) Earth will no longer be considered the only planet inhabited by humanoid life forms.
2) Earth's surface will no longer be considered the only inhabited area of our planet.
3) Because extraterrestrials will represent a truly different species/race of humanoid beings, the concept of race will be redefined and will no

longer apply to humans. Our major ethnic groupings will be given more appropriate designations.
4) ankind's history texts will be revised to include the long-term presence of extraterrestrials.
5) heories of human evolution will be revised to include extraterrestrial intervention in our genetic development.
6) heories of human biology and genetics will be revised to include extraterrestrial genes in our gene pool.

This list will naturally turn out to be much longer, but these few will give you a good idea of the types of changes we should expect.

The Social Impact

Accepting extraterrestrials socially could prove to be more problematic than doing so intellectually, because it would necessitate our willingness to begin considering aliens as co-inhabitants of the Earth and, in a sense, as neighbors. As such, we would also have to keep open the possibility that we could one day live in much closer proximity to them and therefore have increasingly more contact with them. Just think about that for a moment. We sometimes find it hard to tolerate even fellow humans outside of our own national or ethnic groups, so you can imagine how resistant some people are going to be to accepting extraterrestrials as simply another group of fellow Earthlings.

Remember slavery? The attempted genocide of Jewish and other people? The blame for these practices lay squarely on the shoulders of those of us who feared attitude adjustments. When we finally came to our senses and began the adjustments, the social myopia gave way to more open-mindedness, tolerance and inclusiveness. Likewise, when we finally accept the fact that we are not alone in the universe and make the appropriate attitude adjustments, our terrestrial myopia will hopefully yield to a more inclusive and accepting attitude vis-a-vis extraterrestrials. Perhaps the adjustment process could be facilitated by thinking of extraterrestrials as immigrants from a faraway *land*. The bottom line is doing whatever it takes to help adjust our attitudes. Eventually, whether we like it or not, we're all going to have to just get along.

The Spiritual/Religious Impact

The most difficult and potentially painful adjustments of all might well be those involving our spiritual and religious lives. As I mentioned at the beginning of this book, accepting a heliocentric view of our solar system meant that many who lived during the Copernican Revolution had to adjust their spiritual and religious attitudes. Remember, it was the Church's resistance to Galileo's views that led to his house arrest. Why? Because our views about our universe were closely connected with our spiritual beliefs, which are our most deeply rooted attitudes and hence among the most difficult to change.

In a religious sense, our present-day reluctance to believe in UFOs results in part from our reluctance to part with certain remnants of geocentric thinking. For example, our major religions teach that God created Earth as the only life-sustaining planet in the universe–a geocentric attitude. They teach that God's creation of intelligent humanoids was limited to the Earth–another geocentric attitude. The introduction of extraterrestrials into our reality would thus clash with these views and necessitate changes.

Would accepting the reality of UFOs shake the foundations of religion as we know it? Not at all. Religion survived the introduction of a heliocentric view of our world quite nicely. We're adaptable creatures. Just as we've widened the scope of God's plan to include a new system of celestial dynamics, we can widen the scope of His plan to include the implications of humanoid beings from other planets. They too are souls housed in fleshly bodies. They too live under circumstances determined, for the most part, prior to their birth. They too are held divinely accountable for what they do. It's just that they look a little different from most of us and originate from a little farther away than the other continents. Why would this be so difficult to believe? Remember, there are groups of humans living in remote areas of the world that most of us have never seen and would consider very unusual looking; but we would never question their inclusion in God's plan.

Conclusions

Scientifically, we know that other solar systems generally form the same way ours did. That is, after a star, like our sun, forms, its gravitational field normally contains an inner and an outer area of materials that tend to condense and form planetesimals, which in turn, become protoplanets and then mature planets. The outer planets are likely larger and more gaseous like our jovian planets, while the inner ones tend toward smaller size and more solid consistency like our terrestrial planets. And, like our solar system, others will also have a habitable zone where the chances for life to develop are optimal. Out of trillions of such solar systems that form like ours and have habitable zones like ours, why should ours be the only one that has fostered intelligent life? Mathematically speaking, chances are virtually nil that it is.

From a spiritual point of view, why would God have allowed the creation of trillions of solar systems and then limited intelligent life to just one planet in one of them? Yes, the thousands of visible stars that blanket the night sky provide a beautiful spectacle that glorifies God. Yes, stars also have practical functions, such as providing directions for navigation on Earth. Yes, studying stars scientifically aids in our understanding of our own star. But what about the trillions upon trillions of stars and even more planets that are so far away that they are invisible not only to the naked eye, but to our largest telescopes and most sensitive detection instruments? What are they for? Nothing? Allowing so many solar systems like ours to form for no reason at all is like a Detroit car maker assembling a million identical cars for the purpose of one selling one of them. It makes no sense.

But arguments like these don't amount to much unless there is some kind of empirical evidence to back them up. Of course we've seen such evidence during the course of this book. As you recall, this includes the testimony of credible eyewitnesses, physical evidence left behind by UFOs, the myths of virtually every culture around the world, oral and written statements by government officials and millenia of UFO sightings that can't be explained away as hoax or hallucination.

Despite the reasoning and the proof, however, many of us still strongly resist accepting extraterrestrials into our personal and collective spheres of reality. The two main reasons for this are 1) the government's ongoing campaign to withhold the truth about UFOs from the public, and 2) the fear of attitude adjustment. The government's ostensible reasons for continuing its UFO coverups–fear of public panic and disruption of societal systems–are nonsense. We are adaptable beings as we've proven for thousands of years. Once the government changes its official position on UFOs and openly tells us the truth, we will make the necessary attitude adjustments despite our fears to do so. As you recall, the Church had similar fears of accepting the new view of our solar system. When the heliocentric theory became official, and we were forced to either make personal and collective attitude adjustments or reap the stunting consequences of continued ignorance, we chose to adjust. And so it will be when extraterrestrials are officially recognized as integral parts of our reality. For at that time we will not only recognize them as the mythological gods and demons spoken of by our ancestors or the distant relatives that have acted as our guardians since the dawn of civilization, but we will also acknowledge them as fellow spiritual beings created by God and welcome them as another of the many diverse cultures that now dwell on planet Earth.

James Edward Gilmer

Appendix A

Men in Black–Real or Hoax?

Reports of encounters with so-called men in black, or MIBs for short, began in the early 1950's, roughly coinciding with the UFO wave of 1952. The number of such reports has dropped dramatically in recent years. MIBs are said to appear mostly at the homes of people who have seen UFOs or who are otherwise involved with UFO reports. On occasion, they've been seen in other places frequented by their interviewees. Their ostensible reason for visiting someone is normally to investigate a particular sighting and the circumstances surrounding it. In the average report on MIBs, they generally identify themselves as representatives or agents of some organization, usually the federal government. Some say they're from one of the armed services, others from intelligence organizations like the CIA, and still others from organizations that the interviewee has never heard of. Interviewees who have reported a UFO sighting are frequently warned, under clear or implied threats of harm, against saying anything more to anyone about their sighting.

As the phrase 'men in black' suggests, these visitors are reported to wear very dark and often black garments, usually suits. They are generally viewed as odd looking and "foreign" in appearance. Sometimes they are completely hairless, lacking even eyebrows. Although pale at times, MIBs are mostly reported as darker-skinned, ranging from yellowish to dark-brown. They often speak and behave awkwardly, as though new at their jobs. Frequently appearing as a trio, they also come in pairs and even in fours.

Many who are skeptical of the existence of MIBs say they are the result of imagination, hallucination and hoaxes. They say that the fact that MIBs are described in dark clothes is proof that the whole notion is pure fiction, because those who report them associate them with evil and mystery and therefore darkness. There are also those who believe in the reality of MIBs and maintain that eyewitnesses are not hallucinating have no reason to invent their stories.

Ohio, 1967

Robert Richardson of Toledo, Ohio, had a somewhat unusual MIB experience in that he was visited by two different groups of them. It began in July 1967, after a minor collision with a UFO. While driving that night and going around a bend in the road, he saw a large strange-looking object in the middle of the road. He applied the brakes but was too close to avoid some impact with it. A split second later, the object rose and flew away. Richardson immediately notified police, who accompanied him to the site to investigate. They found only his car's skid marks. He returned to the site alone for another look and found a small piece of metal that did not come from his car. Suspecting that it might have broken off the UFO, he showed it confidentially to officials at a UFO research organization called Aerial Phenomena Research Organization (APRO) in Ohio, who kept it for further examination.

Three days later, as midnight approached, two youthful-looking men came to his home and questioned him about the collision. The only things unusual about them were that they were driving a black 1953 Cadillac with an unregistered tag number. That at least showed that they were hiding something. Surprising even himself in retrospect, he recalled after they had left that he had not even asked them what organization they worked for. He just assumed that they were local officials following up on the initial investigation.

A week later, two different men visited him and questioned him on the incident, but this time everything about the men was odd and foreign. In addition, the visitors' remarks included threats. They urged him to forget the collision and to retrieve the piece of metal from APRO or risk harm to his wife. Since only he, his wife and two APRO officials knew about the piece of metal, he wondered how the strangers knew unless they had tapped his phone. He also wondered if there was a connection between the two sets of visitors. Fortunately for him, he received no further visits of this type. Perhaps they realized how frightened Richardson was and felt that his fear would prevent him from telling others about the collision. It did just that, for several years anyway. (Stuttman, vol.16)

France, 1979

This incident was also special among MIB cases, because the person involved didn't just see a UFO, he was also abducted, which is a relative rarity itself. Frank Fontaine, a Frenchman, reported to the police on December 8, that he had been abducted at the beginning of the month and held captive for several days. On the night he was allegedly returned by his captors, he and two of his friends, Solomon and Prevost sat up until the next morning talking about it. Early that morning, there was a knock at the door and Prevost got up to see who it was. When he opened the door, he stood face to face with three men dressed in very dark suits. One wore a beard and was about average height and build. The other two was taller and huskier with hairless faces. The bearded one seemed to be the leader and did all of the talking while the other two stood menacingly by. Everything about them was terrifying. Prevost described their eyes as almost completely white and empty.

The leader asked Prevost if he was one of the three men involved in the UFO abduction case recently reported. After hearing Prevost's affirmative response, he told Prevost to pass the warning to Fontaine and Solomon that, if they said anything further to anyone about the case, they would suffer an accident. The visitors then left. Prevost and his friends saw the strangers on a number of subsequent occasions at other locations. They seemed to know all the places the three friends normally went and would sometimes appear very near one of them, apparently as a silent reminder of their warning. Only on one of those occasions did they orally repeat the threat. The police refused to pursue the visitors, saying that they had not yet done anything wrong.

I think it's interesting that, when Prevost was hypnotized to stimulate his recollection of the MIB encounters, he stated that they were not extraterrestrials, but rather "intraterrestrials." Is there some connection between these MIBs and the intraterrestrials that we discussed in Chapter 7 of this book?

Chariots of Gods or Demons?
The Incredible Truth About UFOs and Extraterrestrials

Appendix B

Sample Government Documents

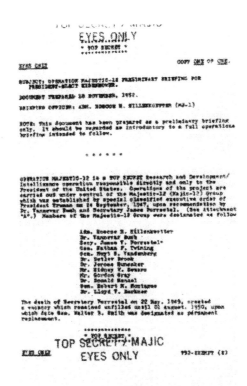

83

(Photocopy of secret Majestic-12 document listing names of members)

James Edward Gilmer

> **TOP SECRET / MAJIC**
> **EYES ONLY**
> * TOP SECRET *
>
> EYES ONLY   COPY ONE O
>
> A covert analytical effort organized by Gen. Twining and Dr. Bush acting on the direct orders of the President, resulted in a preliminary consensus (19 September, 1947) that the disc was most likely a short range reconnaissance craft. This conclusion was based for the most part on the craft's size and the apparent lack of any identifiable provisionin (See Attachment "F".) A similar analysis of the four dead occupants was arranged by Dr. Bronk. It was the tentative conclusion of this group (30 November, 1947) that although these creatures are human-like in appearance, the biologic and evolutionary processes responsible for their developme has apparently been quite different from those observed or postulated in homo-sapiens. Dr. Bronk's team has suggested the term "Extra-terrestrial Biological Entities", or "EBEs be adopted as the standard term of reference for these creatures until such time as a more definitive designation can be agreed upon.
>
> Since it is virtually certain that these craft do not originate in any country on earth, considerable speculation has centered around what their point of origin might be and how they got here. Mars was and remains a possibility, although some scientists, most notably Dr. Menzel, consider it more likely that we are dealing with beings from another solar system entirely.
>
> Numerous examples of what appear to be a form of writing were found in the wreckage. Efforts to decipher these have remained largely unsuccessful. (See Attachment "E".) Equally unsuccessful have been efforts to determine the method of propulsion or the nature or method of transmissi of the power source involved. Research along these lines has been complicated by the complete absence of identifial wings, propellers, jets, or other conventional methods of propulsion and guidance, as well as a total lack of metalli wiring, vacuum tubes, or similar recognizable electronic components. (See Attachment "F".) It is assumed that the propulsion unit was completely destroyed by the explosion which caused the crash.
>
> * TOP SECRET *
> EYES ONLY **TOP SECRET / MAJIC**
> **EYES ONLY**

84

(Photocopy of top secret Majestic-12 document affirming the reality of extraterrestrial crafts and beings)

~~TOP SECRET~~

UNITED STATES DISTRICT COURT
FOR THE DISTRICT OF COLUMBIA

CITIZENS AGAINST UNIDENTIFIED)
FLYING OBJECTS SECRECY,)
)
         Plaintiff,)
)
    v.)   Civil Action No.
)   80-1562
NATIONAL SECURITY AGENCY,)
)
         Defendant.)

IN CAMERA
AFFIDAVIT OF EUGENE F. YEATES

County of Anne Arundel)
) ss:
State of Maryland   )

Eugene F. Yeates, being duly sworn, deposes and says:

1. (U) I am the Chief, Office of Policy, of the National Security Agency (NSA). As Chief, Office of Policy, I am responsible for processing all initial requests made pursuant to the Freedom of Information Act (FOIA) for NSA records. The statements herein are based upon personal knowledge, upon my personal review of information available to me in my official capacity, and upon conclusions reached in accordance therewith.

2. (U) This affidavit supplements my unclassified affidavit executed on September 30, 1980 regarding all documents which have been located by NSA pursuant to plaintiff's FOIA request but which have been withheld wholly or in part by NSA. I submit this affidavit *in camera* for the purpose of stating facts, which cannot be publicly disclosed, that are the basis for exempting the records from release to the plaintiff.

3. (S-█) At the beginning of each paragraph of this affidavit, the letter or letters within parentheses designate(s) the degree of sensitivity of information the paragraph contains.

85

(Photocopy of top secret National Security Agency document regarding the public disclosure of NSA's information on UFOs in response to a FOIA request by the Citizens Against Unidentified Flying Objects Secrecy)

(Photocopy of government document regarding objects that came to be known as ghost rockets)

(Photocopy of Air Force document containing regulations on procedures for reporting UFO activity)

James Edward Gilmer

Appendix C

UFO Organizations–Where to Report Sightings

Aerial Phenomenon Research Organization: Tuscon, Arizona.
APRO: Aerial Phenomenon Research Organization.
British UFO Research Association, London.
BUFORA: British UFO Research Association.
CAUS: Citizens Against UFO Secrecy.
Center for UFO Studies: Evanston, Illinois.
Citizens Against UFO Secrecy: Coventry, Connecticut.
CUFOS: Center for UFO Studies.
Ground Saucer Watch: Phoenix, Arizona.
GSW: Ground Saucer Watch.
International UFO Bureau: Oklahoma City, Oklahoma.
IUB: International UFO Bureau.
MUFON: Mutual UFO Network.
Mutual UFO Network: Atlanta, Georgia; Seguin, Texas; Arizona, Massachusetts, Michigan, Minnesota, Ontario.
National Investigations Committee on Aerial Phenomena: Kensington, Maryland
National UFO Reporting Center: www.ufocenter.com.
NICAP: National Investigations Committee on Aerial Phenomena.
NUFORC: National UFO Reporting Center.
Project Starlight International: Austin, Texas.
PSI: Project Starlight International.
UFO DATABASE.COM.
UFO Report Center: Orange County, California (an affiliate of CUFOS).
URC: UFO Report Center.
UFO Subcommittee of the Committee for the Scientific Investigation of Claims of the Paranormal: Buffalo, New York.
Vehicle Internal Systems Investigative Team: Friendswood, Texas.
VISIT: Vehicle Internal Systems Investigative Team.

James Edward Gilmer

Appendix D

Glossary

AGHARTA: Buddhist name for A legendary subterranean world that was said to be established somewhere beneath the Himalayas about 600,000 years ago and inhabited by beings with special abilities. See Chapter 7: (Agharta).

ALIEN ABDUCTION: The claim that humans are sometimes kidnapped by extraterrestrials and taken aboard UFOs usually for such purposes as medical examinations, and, on occasion, artificial insemination. See Chapter 3: (Close Encounters of the Fourth Kind).

ANTARCTIC CIRCLE: The parallel of latitude that lies at about 66.5 degrees south of the equator and marks the beginning of the southern frigid zone.

ARCTIC CIRCLE: The parallel of latitude that lies about 66.5 degrees north of the equator and marks the beginning of the northern frigid zone.

AREA 51: Government installation near Las Vegas, Nevada, where new aircraft designs and models are developed and tested. Scientists there are also rumored to be engaged in developing various types of devices based on the reverse engineering of UFOs recovered from crash sites. Until recently, the government has denied the existence of Area 51. See Chapter 9: (Area 51 Revealed.)

ASTEROID: Generally speaking, an asteroid is one of the thousands of relatively small rocky bodies that orbit the Sun in the ASTEROID BELT. They have many irregular shapes, those resembling lumpy potatoes.

ASTEROID BELT: Generally speaking, the asteroid belt is the wide band of thousands of ASTEROIDS that orbit the Sun between the orbits of Mars and Jupiter. They are also called minor planets or planetoids and thought by many scientists to be the remains of a "normal" planet that tried to form but was prevented from doing so by the strong disruptive gravitational pull of the gas giant Jupiter. Although the orbits of the vast majority of asteroids in our solar system lie within this belt, there are other "maverick" belts of asteroids, such as the *centaurs* between Jupiter and Saturn and the *trojans* that share Jupiter's orbit.

ATLANTIS: A mythical continent that is said to have existed thousands of years ago before sinking beneath the waves of the ocean that bears its name–the Atlantic. See Chapter 7: (Myths are Based on Reality).

BERMUDA TRIANGLE: The area roughly forming a triangle with points at Bermuda, Miami and Puerto Rico. Also called the devil's triangle, because of the many inexplicable disappearances of ships and planes in this area. See Chapter 7: (Bermuda Triangle).

BIMINI ROAD: A formation of large stones resembling a road underwater near the island of Bimini. Many believe they are remnants of ATLANTIS. See Chapter 7: (Atlantis?).

BIMINI WALL: The formation of large stones considered by many as BIMINI ROAD are also thought to possibly be a fallen wall from ATLANTIS. See Chapter 7: (Atlantis?).

BLACK HOLE: A black hole is what remains of a red supergiant star that has supernovaed and left behind a core so massive that it collapses on itself and becomes so dense that its enormous gravitational pull requires an escape velocity greater than the speed of light. See Chapter 6: (Black Holes and Wormholes).

BLUE HOLES: A system of underwater caves thought by some to have existed above water on ATLANTIS. See Chapter 7: (Atlantis?).

CLOSE ENCOUNTERS: Various levels of close human contact with extraterrestrials normally seen as being of four kinds that increase in levels of closeness:

- A person has *close encounter of the first kind* when he or she sights an unidentified flying object at close range. See Chapter 2: (Close Encounters).
- A *close encounter of the second kind* occurs when some perceptible evidence of a UFO visit is left behind. See Chapter 2: (Close Encounters).
- A *close encounter of the third kind* involves visual contact with the occupants of a UFO. See Chapter 2: (Close Encounters).
- A person who has a *close encounter of the fourth kind* has actual physical contact with occupants of a UFO, most commonly in an ALIEN ABDUCTION. See Chapter 3: (Close Encounters of the Fourth Kind: Abductions).

COMET: A relatively small celestial body composed mainly of ice, dust, and rock. They are generally believed to have formed at the same time as the other main bodies of a solar system, i.e., the sun, planets, and asteroids. The also orbit the sun like the planets and asteroids. As their orbit brings them closer to the sun, the ice begins to thaw, releasing a lot of debris in the form of gas and dust. The comet's bright head and tail is produced when sunlight illuminates the debris.

COSMOLOGY: As a branch of astronomy it refers mainly to the origin, structure, and evolution of the universe. As a branch of metaphysics, it refers chiefly to the origin, structure, and nature of the universe in terms of its innate significance and man's relationship to it.

DEVIL'S TRIANGLE: See BERMUDA TRIANGLE.

DNA: See DEOXYRIBONUCLEIC ACID.

DEOXYRIBONUCLEIC ACID: A nucleic acid found in cellular nuclei, constructed in the shape of a double helix and forming the molecular basis of hereditary in many organisms.

EBE: See EXTRATERRESTRIAL BIOLOGICAL ENTITY.

EVENT HORIZON: The gravitational field around a BLACK HOLE. See Chapter 6: (Black Holes and Wormholes).

EXTRATERRESTRIAL: Originating from a celestial body outside of the Earth.

EXTRATERRESTRIAL BIOLOGICAL ENTITY: A living being of EXTRATERRESTRIAL origin. See Chapter I: (What are UFOs?).

FLAP: A localized period of heightened UFO activity. See Chapter I: (What are UFOs?).

FLYING SAUCER: Although, technically speaking, this term refers only to saucer-shaped UFOs, it has been popularized to the point where it is often used as a synonym for UFO. See Chapter I: (What are UFOs?).

FOIA: FREEDOM OF INFORMATION ACT

FOO FIGHTERS: The term used for UFOs sighted during World War II that were usually described as red or orange globes. See Chapter 4: (Foo Fighters).

FREEDOM OF INFORMATION ACT: Passed in 1966 and reworked in 1974, this act generally provides the legal right for the public to obtain government records. Restrictions are placed on the type of documents obtainable, however, if the release of such information is deemed a risk to national security, as in the case of classified documents.

GALAXY: A large-scale individual unit of stars, gas and dust. Typically a galaxy like our Milky Way will start as a huge shapeless rotating cloud of gas which begins to condense into billions of stars. As the rotation continues, the galaxy often takes the form of a spiral in which older stars occupy the center and younger stars, along with gas and dust, occupy the spiral arms, until the gas and dust gradually disappear.

GAS GIANT: The term used for one of the large OUTER PLANETS in our solar system, which are predominantly composed of gas.

GENETIC INTERVENTION: Intelligently guided external influence on genetic development.

GEOCENTRIC: Literally, the term describes a system or idea that places the Earth at its center. It also describes an older theory of the structure of our known universe that placed the Earth at its center (Contrast HELIOCENTRIC).

GHOST ROCKETS: UFOs sighted in the years immediately following World War II. Although of various shapes and sizes, they were most often described as elongated objects like rockets. See Chapter 4: (Ghost Rockets).

GRAVITATION: A fundamental force of nature that attracts free physical bodies toward each other. Its influence is seen chiefly in the attraction that a larger body exerts on a smaller one.

GREAT LAKES TRIANGLE: The general area of the Great Lakes, with specific reference to the mysterious disappearances of planes and ships in a manner similar to disappearances in the BERMUDA TRIANGLE. See Chapter 7: (The Great Lakes Triangle).

HABITABLE ZONE: The area near the orbits of the Earth and Mars, or, by extension, the same relative area in any typical solar system. See Chapter 6: (The Habitable Zone).

HELIOCENTRIC: A description of a system or idea that places the Sun at its center, sun as a solar system where planets and other bodies revolve around a STAR.

HOMINID: A bipedal primate comprising man, apes, and monkeys.

HUMANOID: Description of a being that has the form and/or other qualities of a human.

HYBRIDIZATION: The genetic mixing or crossing of members of two different species.

HYDROCARBONS: Organic compounds composed of hydrogen and carbon, the largest source of which are coal gas, natural gas, and petroleum.

INNER PLANETS: The planets inside the orbit of the ASTEROID BELT. Contrast with OUTER PLANETS. See Chapter 6: (Which Planets and Moons?).

JAPAN'S DEVIL'S TRIANGLE: The area of the Pacific ocean between Japan and the Marianas Islands where planes and ships mysteriously disappear in a manner similar to disappearances in the BERMUDA TRIANGLE. See Chapter 7: (Japan's Devil's Triangle).

JOVIAN PLANETS: A GAS GIANT; one of the OUTER PLANETS, excluding Pluto.

LIGHT YEAR: The distance light travels through a vacuum in one year, equaling about 5.88 trillion miles.

MAJESTIC-12: A highly secret organization referred to as Majestic-12, MJ-12, and Majic, that is said to have been established in 1947 by President Truman in reaction to the Roswell crash. Its mission was to further explore what happened at the Roswell crash, to research subsequent UFO phenomena, and to report all findings directly to the President. See Chapter 9: (Majestic-12).

METEOR: The bright streak of light we see when a METEOROID flashes across the; often referred to as a "shooting star." The fiery tailed spectacle is caused by the friction generated by the object's flight through a planet's atmosphere.

METEORITE: A larger-scale METEROID that actually does survive its flight through the atmosphere and reaches the Earth's surface. Some are very small by the time they hit the ground and cause little or no surface disruption. Others are very large and create huge craters. The composition of meteorites is usually mostly rock or mostly iron.

METEOROID: A normally small particle of physical matter from outer space that becomes a glowing METEOR when entering a planet's atmosphere.

MITOCHONDRION: A round or oblong energy-producing structure in a cell that contains a different type of DNA from that found in the chromosomes of cellular nuclei. See Chapter 8: (The African Connection).

NEPHILIM: A Hebrew term meaning 'fallen ones', thought by many to refer to extraterrestrials who mated with humans during a period chronicled in the Old Testament book of Genesis. See Chapter 8: (Alien Genetic Intervention?).

OUTER PLANETS: All planets in our solar system whose orbits are outside that of the ASTEROID BELT. Contrast with INNER PLANETS. See Chapter 6: (Which Planets and Moons?).

PLANET: The largest of the physical bodies, usually spherical in shape, that orbit a star. Planets, like those in our own solar system, originate from the interaction of a solar nebula with interstellar microscopic dust particles, which act as seeds around which the nebula gradually condenses until it forms small bodies called planetesimals, which eventually grow to protoplanets and then mature planets. See Chapter 6: (Which Planets and Moons?).

PLANETARY NEBULA: The outer gaseous shell blown away from a red giant star in its death throes. See Chapter 7: (African Dogon Myths).

PLUGHOLE: A large circular opening in the lunar surface believed by some to lead to sub-surface spaces. See Chapter 6: (The Enigmatic Moon).

PROJECT BLUE BOOK: A government project for investigating UFOs. See Chapter 9: (Project Blue Book).

PROJECT GRUDGE: A government project for investigating UFOs. See Chapter 9: (Project Grudge).

PROJECT SIGN: A government project for investigating UFOs. See Chapter 9: (Project Sign).

RED GIANT: A low-mass star about the size of our Sun in its latter stages of a relatively long life, which swells up in preparation for a violent death. See Chapter 7: (African Dogon Myths).

RED SUPERGIANT: A high-mass star–at least 15 times larger than our Sun– in the latter stages of a relatively short life, swelling up in its death throes and eventually dying in a supernova blast. See Chapter 6: (Black Holes and Wormholes).

REGOLITH: The dusty surface of a solid planet or moon. See Chapter 6: (The Enigmatic Moon).

ROSWELL CRASH: The famous 1947 crash of an object near Roswell, New Mexico, that many insist was a UFO. See Chapter 4: (The Roswell Crash).

SHAMBHALA: The capital city of AGHARTA. See Chapter 7: (Agharta).

SOLAR SYSTEM: A star holding a group of celestial bodies in orbit by gravitational attraction.

SPACE-TIME: A dimensional system like ours that is composed of three spatial and one temporal dimension. See Chapter 6: (Interdimensional Travel).

SPHINX: A huge Egyptian statue portraying a mythical monster with a lion's body and human head and positioned as a guardian of the pyramids of Giza. See Chapter 8: (Testimony by the Sphinx?).

STAR: Stars are born after the particles in cosmic gas clouds condense due to gravitation, eventually forming clusters of matter that continue to grow, simultaneously creating heat-producing friction that gradually increases to the point where a nuclear furnace is created in the core of the embryonic star, aka protostar, which eventually becomes a mature star.

SINGULARITY: The dense remainder of a massive stellar core collapse. See Chapter 6: (Black Holes and Wormholes).

TERRESTRIAL PLANETS: The planets that are closest to our Sun and that orbit our solar system inside the orbit of the ASTEROID BELT. See Chapter 6: (The Terrestrial Planets). INNER PLANETS.

THERMAL DRILL: A drill that bores into the earth by melting rocks See Chapter 7: (Can Aliens Dig Underground Without Being Discovered?)

UFO: An unidentified flying object. See Chapter I: (What Are UFOs?).

WAVE: A period of heightened UFO activity over an extended region and time frame. See Chapter I: (What Are UFOs?).

WHITE DWARF: This is the hot core that remains of a low-mass star, which, in its death throes has swollen to a RED GIANT and then blown off its outer layers. See Chapter 7: (African Dogon Myths).

WHITE HOLE: The theoretical exit point for what enters a BLACK HOLE. See Chapter 6: (Black Holes, White Holes and Wormholes).

WORMHOLE: A theoretical conduit or tunnel through the space-time fabric of our known universe. See Chapter 6: (Black Holes, White Holes and Wormholes).

Bibliography

Berlitz, Charles, *Mysteries From Forgotten Worlds*. New York: Dell Publishing Co., Inc., 1972.

Berlitz, Charles, *The Bermuda Triangle*. New York: Avon Books, 1975.

Berlitz, Charles, *Without A Trace*. New York: Doubleday and Company, Inc., 1977.

Bernard, Raymond Dr., *The Hollow Earth*. New York: Bell Publishing Company, 1979.

Blum, Ralph with Judy Blum, *Beyond Earth: Man's Contact With UFOs*. New York: Bantam Books, Inc., 1974.

Blumrich, Josef F., *The Spaceships of Ezekiel*. New York: Bantam Books, Inc., 1974.

Bowen, Charles, *The Humanoids*. Chicago: Henry Regnery Company, 1969.

Charroux, Robert, *Masters of The World*. New York: Berkeley Publishing Corporation, 1974.

Childress, David Hatcher, *Extraterrestrial Archaeology*. Illinois: Adventures Unlimited Press, 1994.

CNI News (Paranormal Internet Site).

Commander X, *Underground Alien Bases*. Abelard Productions, 1990.

Corso, Philip J., *The Day After Roswell*. New York: Pocket Books, 1997.

Cragg, Dan, *Guide to Military Installations*. Mechanicsburg, Pa.: Stackpole Books, 1997.

Crowley, Brian and James Hurtak, *The Face on Mars: Evidence of a Lost Martian Civilization*.
Melbourne: Sun Publishing Company, 1986.

Fawcett, Lawrence and Barry Greenwood, *Clear Intent*. Englewood Cliffs: Prentice-Hall, Inc., 1984.

Fowler, Raymond E., *UFOs: Interplanetary Visitors*. Jericho: Exposition Press, Inc., 1974.

Frederick, Robert, A la Recherche des Extra-Terrestres. Paris: Bordas Poche, 1973.

Gadd, Laurence D., *The Second Book of the Strange*. New York: World Almanac, 1981.

Good, Timothy, *Above Top Secret*. New York: William Morrow and Company, Inc., 1988.

Hammerton, Sir John and Harry Elmer Barnes, *The Illustrated World History*. New York: William H. Wise & Co., 1939.

Hoagland, Richard, *The Monuments of Mars*. Berkeley: North Atlantic Books, 1987.

International Masters Publishers, *Secrets of The Universe*. USA, 1997.

Jacobs, David Michael, *The UFO Controversy in America*. Bloomington: Indiana University Press, 1975.

Jeffrey, Adi-Kent Thomas, *The Bermuda Triangle*. New York: Warner Paperback Library, 1975.

Kolosimo, Peter, *Not of This World*. New York: Bantam Books, 1973.

Kolosimo, Peter, *Timeless Earth*. New York: Bantam Books, 1975.

Landsburg, Alan, *In Search of Extraterrestrials*. New York: Bantam Books, 1977.

Le Poer Trench, Brinsley., *The Flying Saucer Story*. New York: Ace Books, 1966.

Luce, J.V., *Lost Atlantis*. New York: McGraw-Hill Book Company, 1969.

Marrs, Jim. *Alien Agenda*, New York: HarperCollins Publishers, Inc., 1997.

National Geographic Society, *The Mysterious Maya*. Washington, D.C., 1983.

Outexcel! Corporation, *Navigating The Universe*. New York, 1998.

Paranet (Paranormal Internet Site).

Poignant, Roslyn, *Oceanic Mythology*. New York: Hamlyn Publishing Group Limited, 1967.

Pope, Nick, *Open Skies, Closed Minds*. New York: Dell Publishing Company, 1998.

Randle, Kevin D. and Donald R. Schmitt, *UFO Crash at Roswell*. New York: Avon Books, 1991.

Reader's Digest Editors, *Mysteries of the Unexplained*. New York: Reader's Digest Association, Inc., 1990.

Sauder, Richard, *Underground Bases and Tunnels*. Kempton: Adventures Unlimited Press, 1995.

Spencer, John Wallace, Limbo of The Lost. New York: Bantam Books, 1973

Steiger, Brad, *Atlantis Rising*. New York: Dell Publishing Company, Inc., 1973.

Steiger, Brad and Sherry Hansen Steiger, *UFO Odyssey*. New York: Ballantine Books, 1999.

Story, Ronald D., *The Encyclopedia of UFOs*. New York: Doubleday and Company, Inc., 1980.

Stuttman, H.S., *Mysteries of Mind Space & Time*. Westport: H.S. Stuttman, Inc., 1992.

Time Life Books, *Feats and Wisdom of the Ancients*. Alexandria, Va., 1990

Tomas, Andrew, *We Are Not The First*. New York: Bantam Books, 1971.

UFO Roundup 1996-2000 (UFO Internet site).

Vallee, Jacques, *Anatomy of a Phenomenon*. Chicago: Henry Regnery Company, 1965

Vallee, Jacques, *Passport to Magonia*. Chicago: Henry Regnery Company, 1969.

Von Daeniken, Erich, Chariots of the Gods? New York: Bantam Books, 1971.

Von Daeniken, Erich, *Gold of the Gods*. Ontario: Souvenir Press, 1973.

Von Daeniken, Erich, *In Search of Ancient Gods*. New York: Bantam Books, 1975.

Von Daeniken, Erich, *Von Daeniken's Proof*. New York: Bantam Books, 1978.

Wilkins, Harold, *Flying Saucers on the Attack*. New York: Citadel Press, 1954.

Willis, Roy, *World Mythology*. New York: Henry Holt and Company, Inc., 1996.

Credits for Compiled Photos, Illustrations and Documents

Figure 1:	Reader's Digest
Figure 2:	Author
Figure 3:	Stuttman
Figure 4:	Reader's Digest, Fowler
Figures 5-7:	Stuttman
Figure 8:	Reader's Digest
Figures 9, 10:	Stuttman
Figure 11:	Reader's Digest
Figures 12, 13:	Frederick
Figure 14:	Reader's Digest
Figure 15:	Reader's Digest
Figure 16:	Gadd
Figures 17-20:	Stuttman
Figure 21:	Blum
Figure 22:	Corso
Figure 23:	Reader's Digest
Figure 24:	Randle
Figure 25:	Time Magazine, 20 June 1997
Figure 26:	Reader's Digest
Figure 27:	Good
Figures 28, 29:	Reader's Digest
Figure 30:	Stuttman
Figure 31:	International Masters
Figure 32:	International Masters
Figure 33:	Landsburg
Figure 34:	Landsburg
Figure 35:	Reader's Digest
Figure 36:	Hammerton
Figures 37, 38:	Reader's Digest
Figures 39-41:	Blumrich
Figures 42-44:	International Masters
Figures 45-47:	Childress
Figure 48:	Good
Figure 49:	Outexcel!
Figures 50, 51:	Childress
Figure 52:	Outexcel!

Figure 53:	Reader's Digest
Figures 54, 55:	Spencer
Figure 56:	Luce
Figure 57:	Berlitz, 1977
Figure 58:	International Masters
Figure 59:	Stuttman
Figure 60:	Time-Life Books
Figure 61:	Berlitz, 1972
Figure 62:	Stuttman
Figure 63:	Landsburg
Figure 64:	Stuttman
Figure 65:	Berlitz, 1975
Figure 66:	Stuttman
Figure 67:	Hammerton
Figures 68-72:	Good
Figures 73, 74:	Baltimore Sun, April 2000
Figures 75, 76:	Randle
Figures 77, 78:	Good
Figure 79:	Corso
Figures 80, 81:	Stuttman
Figures 82-85:	Fawcett
Figure 86:	Good

About The Author

James Edward Gilmer is a certified hypnotherapist who holds A. A., B. S., M. A., M. Ed., and Ph.D. degrees from several colleges and universities. A polyglot who has studied in various countries around the world, Dr. Gilmer has taught foreign languages and served as a translator-interpreter for the federal government. He has done extensive research on paranormal phenomena, which has formed the basis of earlier books of his including *Brothers in the Light*, A book on near-death experiences, and *For a Hundred Lifetimes*, a reincarnation romance novel - both books were published by 1stBooks Library.

CPSIA information can be obtained
at www.ICGtesting.com
Printed in the USA
LVOW07*2330310817
547186LV00003B/23/P